100 Instant Children's Talks

SUE RELF

KINGSWAY PUBLICATIONS
EASTBOURNE

First published 1994
Reprinted 1994, 1995

ISBN 0 85476 388 0

Produced by Bookprint Creative Services
P.O. Box 827, BN21 3YJ, England for
KINGSWAY PUBLICATIONS LTD
Lottbridge Drove, Eastbourne, E. Sussex, BN23 6NT

100 Instant Children's Talks

SECTION ONE

General Talks

1. *The Language of the Sky*

Bible references:	Psalm 19:1–4; Romans 1:20
Teaching point:	Everyone should know that God is very great simply by looking up at the sky
Equipment needed:	Four cardboard cut-out 'speech bubbles': 'God is great', 'God is wonderful', 'God is glorious' and 'God is powerful' written on them

Contents

Introduction

Jesus was praying fervently for his disciples before he was taken away from them. He asked his Father to 'sanctify them by the truth', and added, 'Your word is truth' (John 17:17). I believe the whole Bible is God's life-giving message to men and women—the means by which they will be 'sanctified'.

Boys and girls need to be sanctified too! They need to know the true word of God, and appropriate means of communicating it are essential if they are really to 'hear it'. This is a book for busy people who want to teach God's truth to children.

Children's talks are needed to fit many different situations—church services, family services, school assemblies, Bible clubs, holiday clubs and missions, regular children's activities and so on. I hope that there are ideas here that can be fitted into all of these. The talks are not intended to be slavishly followed; they can be adapted, embellished, shortened, developed or altered in whatever way is necessary in order to make them suitable for the age and background of the children and the situation in which to talk is to be given.

According to tradition, a sermon has three points; a children's talk must have only one! It needs to be simple and its message clear if it is to be effective. Permission is given for the cartoons at the beginning of each talk to be enlarged onto an overhead projector acetate to reinforce the message if desired.

Bible references are included for each talk. These can be brought in in several ways: everyone can read together; readers can be chosen beforehand; someone can be asked in advance to put a verse or passage into their own words; the same verse can be read in different versions so that it is heard several times; a verse can be displayed on an overhead projector so that it is seen as well as heard, and can be referred to later; if it is short it can be written out on large cards and assembled like a jigsaw as an activity at some point.

I have made suggestions for songs which might be used for each occasion, and these are taken from four different songbooks; *Songs of Fellowship for Kids* (SFK), published by Kingsway; *Junior Praise* (JP), published by Marshall Pickering; *Sing to God* (SG), published by Scripture Union; and *Come and Praise* (CP); published by the BBC.

Nothing in this world is really 'instant' (even Angel Delight has to be mixed with milk), but these talks have been designed bearing in mind ingredients that are already 'in the cupboard'. The items that will be needed are paper and pens, clothes, or common household items. An overhead projector is an advantage, but by no means essential. I wish you well with them.

Sue Relf

Has anyone heard the sky speaking recently? Walk to a window, look out and cup your hand behind your ear as though you were listening intently. Tell everyone you can hear the sky speaking very loudly and clearly. Can anyone guess what it is saying?

Ask someone to look up and read Psalm 19:1–4.

Show your 'speech bubbles' and get four volunteers to hold them up and repeat in a loud voice what the sky is saying.

Every single day that passes, the message that God is glorious is declared from one end of the world to the other. Everybody in the whole world can see the sky night and day, and something deep inside each person tells them that God is there and that he is great.

When we look up at the sky do we hear its message? Yes, we do! Repeat the chosen phrases once more with everyone joining in.

Songs: *From the rising of the sun* (SFK)
This is the day (SFK) (JP)
All around me, Lord (JP)
All creatures of our God and King (SG) (CP)
All the nations of the earth (CP)

2. *How Does Your Garden Grow?*

Bible references: Mark 4:26–29; Philippians 1:6

Teaching point: God's kingdom will inevitably grow

Equipment needed: A tray of soil and a packet of seeds

Show the seeds. Talk about their size and shape. What is needed to make them grow? They will not grow without soil, moisture and light. However, these things in themselves do not have the power to make the seeds grow. They grow because God has put a life force within them.

Look together at the parable Jesus told in Mark 4. Jesus said the kingdom of God was like the planting of these seeds. We do not know how it happens, but God's seed in our hearts grows and grows. God's seed in the world is growing and growing. God has given his kingdom a living force which means it is bound to grow.

Songs: *All over the world* (SFK) (JP)
I've got the life of God in me (SFK)
God is working his purpose out (JP)
With the Father when the world began (SG)
Light up the fire (CP)

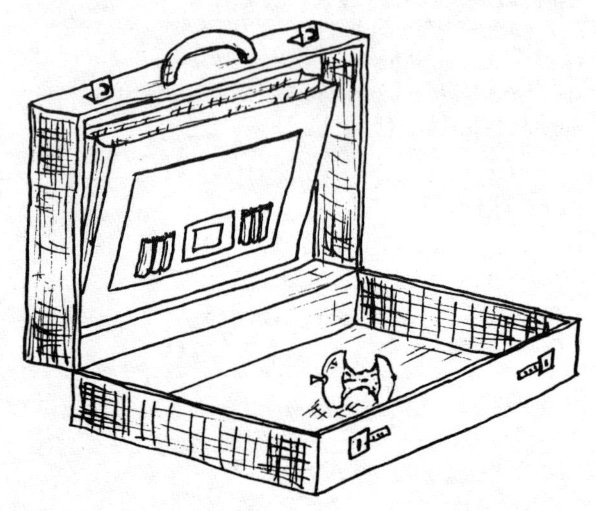

3. *Look Inside*

Bible references:	1 Samuel 16:7; Matthew 23:27
Teaching point:	God is concerned about a person's heart and takes no notice of appearance or status
Equipment needed:	As many smart-looking black executive brief-cases as you can borrow; inside each one place a clear plastic bag with something unsavoury in it, such as a squashed tomato, an old sandwich or a broken biscuit; a well-worn, old-fashioned brief-case; inside this case put a wallet

Talk about executive brief-cases and the image that they convey, pretending that you have always wanted one. Compare the smartness of the cases you have borrowed and take a walk with each one, looking very important and pleased with yourself. Make fun of the old brief-case.

Open each case in turn and express horror as you reveal the contents. Pick up the old-fashioned brief-case and say how this old thing could not possibly contain anything interesting. Open it and take out the wallet with complete amazement. Who would have thought it? Something really valuable inside an old case like this? It just goes to show that you cannot judge by appearances! What kind of 'appearances' do people judge others by—clothes, looks, bikes, hairstyle, cars?

Read or tell the story in 1 Samuel 16. God sees into a person's mind and heart and is neither impressed nor put off by someone's outside appearance.

Songs: *I want to walk with Jesus Christ* (SFK) (JP)
My Lord my God, I know you see (SG)
Make me a channel of your peace (CP) (JP)

4. *The Answer Lies in the Soil*

Bible reference: Luke 8:5–15

Teaching point: It is the condition of our hearts towards God that is important (the parable of the sower)

Equipment needed: Four garden pots—one with the soil dry and tightly packed down, one filled with stones with a dusting of soil, one with a plant already in it and one filled with rich, well-prepared soil; some seeds

Tell the parable of the sower from Luke 8:5–15 and show your pots one by one to demonstrate where the seeds fell.

Tell the story of the parable again, referring to God's word and the type of hearts that each pot represents.

How important it is to make sure that we have responsive and listening hearts from an early age, so that the seed of God's word can grow in us and produce lots of fruit!

Songs: *Hang on* (SFK)
I want to live for Jesus every day (JP)
The Sower (SG)
Fill your hearts with joy (CP)

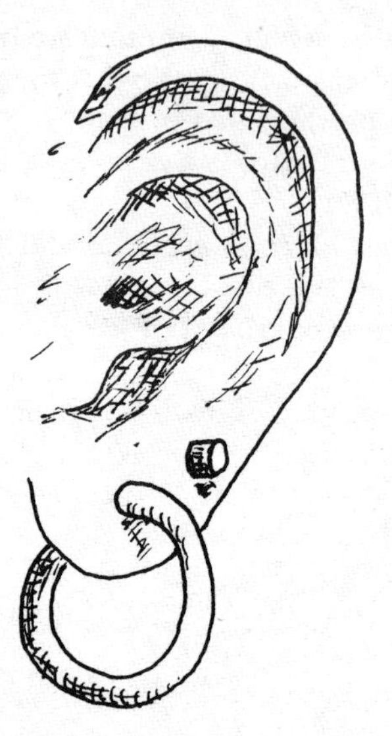

5. *Keep Listening*

Bible references: Hebrews 1:1–2, 3:7; Psalm 19:1–4

Teaching point: We must listen when God speaks

Equipment needed: Tape recorder and any music tape; short poem to read

Talk about 'listening tests'. Who has ever taken part in one? What different kinds of listening tests are there? Explain that you have a listening test for everyone now.

Play your chosen piece of music—about thirty seconds' worth is a good length of time. When it has finished, move straight on to the poem and read it through.

How many people listened to all the music without losing concentration or thinking their own thoughts at least once? Get them to raise their hands, telling them you are trusting them to be really honest with you.

Next, ask those who listened to the poem all the way through to raise their hands. How many people listened to all the music and all the poem? Who listened to neither all the way through?

We can have perfect ears for hearing and yet do very little listening!

God has given us 'spiritual ears'. These sorts of 'ears' are inside our hearts and minds and our consciences. God wants to speak to us, and it is very important that we listen carefully with our inner 'ears' open.

Ask the children to give examples of the sorts of things which God might say. Does anyone have an example of a time when God spoke to them? Have an example of your own ready.

Sadly, many people are switched off to God and never hear him say a word. How important it is to listen to God's voice!

Songs: *Let God speak and I will listen* (SFK)
Isaiah heard the voice of the Lord (JP)
Somebody's knocking (SG)
A still small voice (CP)

6. *Possible or Impossible?*

Bible references: Luke 18:24–30; Matthew 6:24

Teaching point: It is impossible to live for both God and money

Equipment needed: A sewing needle; some rope or thick string

Begin by asking if anyone has a good eye for threading needles. Choose a volunteer before revealing the size of the task.

Ask if anyone can remember in what context Jesus talked about threading needles. Refer to the story in Luke 18 where Jesus was talking about trying to get a camel through the eye of a needle. (Tell them you couldn't get hold of a camel so you've brought a rope instead!)

What comparison was Jesus making? Discuss some of the reasons why rich people might find it difficult to start the Christian life. (However, Jesus said it was not impossible.)

Encourage the youngsters to see that having many possessions can be a big hindrance to entering God's kingdom. It is not possible to live both for God and for money.

Songs: *Seek ye first* (SFK) (JP)
I have decided to follow Jesus (SFK) (JP)
Choose you this day (SG)
The King of love (CP)

7. *A Stain Is a Stain*

Bible references: Romans 3:23; Luke 18:9–14

Teaching point: All are sinners to one degree or another and need their sins forgiven

Equipment needed: A white shirt or blouse stained with a (washable!) ink blot in the front which can be concealed naturally by an arm or jumper, but which can be made clearly visible

Open a conversation about something trivial, like the weather, revealing the stain in mid-sentence as though you were not aware of its presence. Then stop and ask what is wrong. When the stain is pointed out, act as though you think it is very unimportant since it is only a small stain and the rest of the shirt is perfectly clean. Ask the children for their opinions on the matter.

Explain how sin spoils the whole of our lives, even though it may seem small to us. It is no good trying to cover it up or to pretend it is not there.

Tell or read the story of the Pharisee and the tax collector in Luke 18:10-14.

Admitting our sinfulness and asking for forgiveness is the only way to be acceptable before God.

Songs: *Grace is* (SFK)
I get so excited, Lord (SFK)
O happy day (JP)
There's a way back to God (SG)
The Lord's prayer (CP)

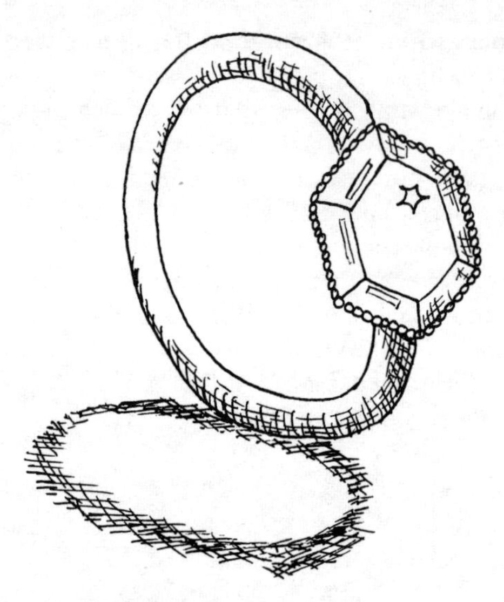

8. *Lost or Found?*

Bible reference: Luke 15:1–10

Teaching point: God loves people to turn to him in repentance

Equipment needed: Something quite small and valuable, such as your wedding ring, or an imitation, which you have previously hidden somewhere

Begin your talk by pretending to be very upset about your missing ring. Make up a plausible story about how it came to be lost and send the children on a search party to help find it. Go out searching with them. You may need to give clues as to where you might have 'dropped' it!

Pretend to be extremely relieved and happy when it is found and say how Jesus told two very similar stories 2,000 years ago.

Ask for a volunteer to read the story of the lost sheep in Luke

15, and another to read the story of the lost coin. Was Jesus really talking about sheep and coins? No! He was talking about people like you and me!

These stories tell us how much God loves and values individual people. It was not any old coin or sheep that was lost, but particular ones. Jesus said that when we turn from our old way of life to follow Jesus, the angels in heaven rejoice over us! When each one here today started his or her new life in Jesus there was rejoicing in heaven! Imagine a celebration in heaven just for you or me!

Songs: *Shout for joy and sing* (SFK)
God is good (SFK) (JP)
I was lost (JP)
He laid down his life (SG)
God who made the earth (CP)

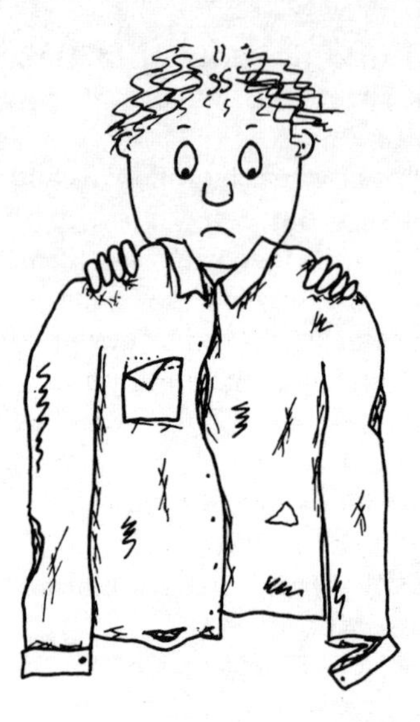

9. *Don't Put Your Shirt on It!*

Bible references: Isaiah 64:6; Luke 10:27–28; Romans 3:22–23

Teaching point: God does not accept me because of my good deeds. I need to be forgiven

Equipment needed: An old shirt which can be thrown away afterwards, smeared with dirty marks and with slashes or holes

Pretend that this week you have been trying hard to be an especially good person. Pretend that you have put a lot of effort into this, and tell of one or two things you have done—like washing up once, or putting 50p in a collection box, or other such minor good deeds. Continue your story by pretending that as a reward for being such a good person you are to get a new shirt.

Arrange in advance for someone to bring you the shirt in a

carrier bag at this point. Take it out of the bag with great anticipation. Then put it on over your other clothes.

What a disappointment! Is this your reward for your good deeds? There must be some mistake. . .or is there? Ask for a volunteer to read Isaiah 64:6.

In God's eyes our little good deeds are like 'filthy rags'. We can never be good enough. He wants us to obey two commandments. Read Luke 10:27–28. First, he wants us to live in perfect relationship with him, and second, he wants us to live in perfect relationships with everyone else. Perhaps my 'good deeds' are like filthy rags after all. They certainly do not get anywhere near obeying these two commandments.

As you take off the shirt, explain that while 'good deeds' are great, the only way to be accepted by God is to believe in Jesus and receive his total forgiveness.

Songs: *Thank you for the cross* (SFK)
He paid a debt (JP)
Come and praise (SG)
When Jesus walked in Galilee (CP)

10. *A Real Change*

Bible reference: 2 Corinthians 5:17

Teaching point: Those who put their trust in Christ start a completely new life

Equipment needed: A complete change of clothes

You will need to dress yourself in two sets of clothes beforehand. Wear something that contrasts completely with your usual style of dress, then put your ordinary clothes over the top. The outfit underneath should not be visible. Accessories like a hat, sunglasses, visor, gloves and another pair of shoes, can be brought to complete your change of image.

Begin your talk by pretending that you are feeling fed up with your life. Talk about yourself in a depressed way, emphasising poor qualities of your character or unhappy circumstances.

Then, as though you have suddenly had an idea, announce that you have decided to change. You are going to become a different person. Begin to unbutton your shirt and discard your 'top' set of clothes. Complete your image change. How does everyone like the new you?

Is this a real change, though? Nothing, except your clothes, has really changed. You are still exactly the same person.

The Bible tells us something quite amazing in 2 Corinthians 5:17. If we are in Christ, then we are a new creation! We are transformed on the inside by Jesus when we commit our lives to him. He makes a real change and it lasts for ever!

Songs: *I am a new creation* (SFK)
There's new life in Jesus (JP)
With the Father when the world began (SG)
From darkness came light (CP)

11. Everything Provided

Bible references: Mark 8:34; Matthew 13:44–45

Teaching point: Following Jesus is always more important than looking to my own needs and interests.

Equipment needed: A small suitcase; a coat and scarf; a purse, wallet or cheque book; a popular music cassette or CD; a family photograph; a football club scarf or similar fanclub regalia

Announce that you are off on the journey of your life. Can anyone guess where you are going? No, not Disneyworld, Disneyland or Eurodisney—somewhere much more exciting: heaven! Tell the youngsters that you have received your ticket and you are off to check in at the airport.

Let the children watch you as you pack your suitcase. Make a running commentary on each item you put in, giving the reasons why each one is so important and why you are including it in your suitcase. (Include any other items which are suited to your situation.)

When you are ready, shut the case and emphasise that you have been told that you were not allowed to bring anything with you, as everything you will need is to be provided. However, you feel confident that one small case will be acceptable. Put on your scarf and coat and walk to a suitable table, then pretend to check in with the imaginary official. Turn to the children and look horrified. You've been told you are not allowed through unless you leave the case behind. Rehearse the pros and cons as you make the decision. How will you manage without your favourite music? Can you really leave your money behind? Pick up the case and put it down several times as though you were agonising over the decision.

Finally, put the case down and hurriedly walk on, making comments like: 'A window seat? How wonderful! Jesus himself will be sitting next to me? This is fantastic! Just to think I could have missed all this!'

Songs: *I lift my hands* (SFK)
The greatest thing (JP)
Jesus supreme in my heart (SG)
I am planting my feet (CP)

12. *Nothing to Be Afraid Of*

Bible references:	Psalm 49; John 11:25
Teaching point:	Everyone dies; Jesus is the only way to beat death
Equipment needed:	Obituaries from a newspaper

Read out an obituary slowly. Look up and tell the children the date of the newspaper you are reading. Make observations like: 'I wonder what he did during his life,' or, 'I wonder how rich he was.' Continue reading one or two more, making other comments about the age at death of the deceased, or highlighting items that are mentioned. Every day, the newspapers have obituaries like these.

How does this make you feel? Every one of us will die one day, just like these people. It may be a long way off, but our turn will come! Read some verses from Psalm 49 if desired.

However, we need have no fear. Jesus has conquered death! For those who believe in him, death is like a doorway to eternal life! Look up John 11:25.

Songs: *The Lord will rescue me* (SFK)
What a wonderful Saviour is Jesus (SFK) (SG)
I will sing the wondrous story (JP)
The Lord's my shepherd (CP)

13. *The Holiday of a Lifetime!*

Bible references: Revelation 4; 7:9–17; 21:1–4; John 14:2–3

Teaching point: Heaven is a wonderful place

Equipment needed: Travel brochures of exotic places

Introduce the subject of travelling and foreign holidays. Pick up one of your brochures and describe how marvellous a certain place sounds with its miles of golden beaches, and so on.

Follow on by saying that the brochures tell us enough to whet our appetites and make us want to go to the place they are describing. (Sometimes people find they have been led astray!)

Parts of the Bible are like a travel brochure. We are given glimpses of what heaven is like. We can trust completely what the Bible says. It makes travelling around the world sound very dull by comparison. Read out a selection of verses from the above Bible passages to whet the appetite.

Songs: *O, heaven is in my heart* (SFK)
Soon and very soon (JP)
We are marching home (SG)
The Lord's my shepherd (CP)

SECTION TWO

God the Father

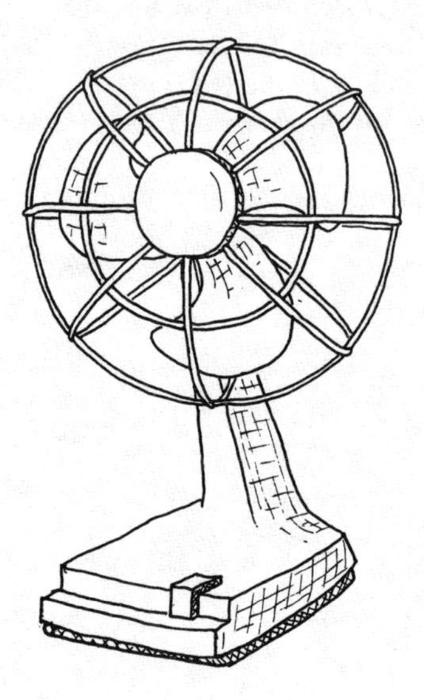

14. God Is Invisible

Bible references: 1 Timothy 1:17; Romans 1:20

Teaching point: God is not visible, but he is real

Equipment needed: Bellows or fan

Talk about air. What is it? Where is it? Why do we need it? Which of our senses detects it?

We do not have to see air to know that it is there. It is invisible, but that makes no difference to its reality. Although we do not see air, we can see its effects. We know that we breathe it in and out. A hand on the chest will feel the slight movement of our lungs up and down. However, much of the time we are totally unconscious of the air around us and unconscious of breathing.

With the fan or bellows give the children the feel of a breeze on their faces. Now they are conscious of the air.

When the air is still we do not doubt that it is there. Some days it is windy and we are more conscious of it. Sometimes God seems to be very 'still' and we do not see anything happening. Maybe then we wonder if he is real at all. However, God is still there. He will always be there. And sometimes God does very dramatic things and we see the effects very noticeably.

What are some of the effects of the things that God does?

Songs: *God's not dead* (SFK) (JP)
Be still and know (JP) (SFK)
O God of faith (SG)
Praise him (CP)

15. Both Three and One

Bible reference: John 14:8–20

Teaching point: God is one, and at the same time he is three

Equipment needed: A thermos with a block of ice in it; an electric kettle with enough water to cover the element; a heavy duty extension lead; a cup

Talk about water in general terms. (Look in an encyclopedia for scientific/geographical facts if desired.) Produce the ice from the thermos and heat it in the kettle until some steam appears.

Pour some water into the cup. Carefully remove the remains of the ice. All of these three are exactly the same substance but they are quite distinct and separate from each other.

We learn from the Bible that God is himself in three different persons. It is hard to imagine it, but he is God the Father, God the Son and God the Holy Spirit. Each of them is distinct and separate, but each of them is God.

Perhaps we can think of God like the water, ice and steam? God is one, and at the same time he is three.

Songs: *Heavenly Father, I appreciate you* (SFK)
Father, we love you (JP)
Praise God from whom all blessings flow (SG) (JP)
All creatures of our God and King (CP)

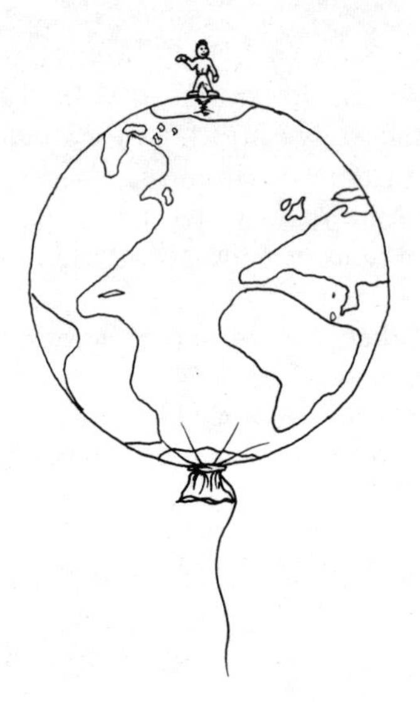

16. Mega God—and Micro Me

Bible reference: Matthew 10:29

Teaching point: God is infinitely powerful and vast

Equipment needed: A round balloon and a dried pea

Ask a volunteer to blow up and knot the balloon. (Have a spare one in hand in case of accidents!) Holding the balloon in one hand and the pea in the other, ask the children, using the relative size of the balloon and the pea, to compare themselves in size with the room you are in. Each individual is like the pea, and the room is like the balloon. But if the room itself is then compared with the town or district you live in, the room becomes the pea.

Continue in a similar way, asking the children to compare the size of the town you live in and the county, then the county and the UK, then the UK and the world, then the world and the sun, then the sun and the solar system, then the solar system and the Milky Way, and finally the Milky Way and the universe.

As you work up through the steps in size, every so often remind the youngsters of where you started—with the size of each individual compared to the size of the room.

Finally, compare the universe with God who made it. The universe is like the pea and God is like the balloon. How great God is and how small I am! He loves and cares for me, even though I am a tiny speck. If you compare your size to a sparrow, which is like the balloon and which is like the pea? Matthew 10:29 tells us he sees even a tiny sparrow fall to the ground. How he must care for us!

Songs: *Who's the king of the jungle?* (SFK) (JP)
My God is so big (SFK) (JP)
There are hundreds of sparrows (JP) (SG) (CP)

17. *God Is a Genius*

Bible references: Genesis 1:1; Psalm 104:24

Teaching point: God made the world with fantastic ingenuity and skill

Equipment needed: The bottom six inches of an empty washing up liquid bottle; glue; coloured tissue paper; newspaper for protection; some flowers to put in the vase when it is finished

Show the bottom half of the plastic bottle, the tissue paper and the glue, and ask how many items these are. You have thought of one thing that could be made using these three items: a vase. Ask for one or two volunteers to come forward and make a vase by tearing the tissue paper into small pieces and sticking them haphazardly around the outside of the bottle.

While this is in progress, continue by describing how God has used only three items not to make just one thing but to create the whole universe. He designed and made three microscopic building blocks, and by fitting them together in fantastic numbers with his mighty power and skill, he has made everything we see. How can it be possible?

It is perfectly true. The three building blocks are: protons, neutrons and electrons. Every atom of every substance consists of these same three in different combinations. Atoms themselves are so small that one billion in a line would measure only one centimetre, so how minute are protons, neutrons and electrons!

Point to some contrasting objects and ask what they are made of. Protons, neutrons and electrons. Nothing else.

Have the volunteers finished the vase? Put your flowers into it. These beautiful flowers consist purely of trillions of protons, neutrons and electrons! God is nothing short of a genius!

Songs: *The earth is the Lord's* (SFK)
He made the earth (SFK)
All things bright and beautiful (JP) (SG) (CP)

18. *He Names Them One by One*

Bible references: Psalm 147:4–5; Isaiah 40:26

Teaching point: God is greater than we can possibly imagine

Equipment needed: None

Ask if anyone knows which star is nearest to the earth. The answer, of course, is the sun. Next, ask if anyone knows which galaxy the sun (and we on the earth) belong to. The answer is the Milky Way. Does anyone know how many stars there are in the Milky Way? The answer is approximately one hundred thousand million. How incredible!

Of course, the Milky Way is only one of many galaxies. With the aid of the most powerful telescopes it is possible to see several thousand million galaxies stretching out in all directions. They extend beyond the limit of the telescopes, beyond the ability of light to travel from them to the earth, so no one knows when they end. Several thousand million galaxies each with millions of stars, and maybe millions more which we cannot see!

What does Psalm 147:4–5 say? Can you believe it? God has decided on the number of stars and calls each one by name!

Read verse 5 together as an act of worship.

Songs: *He made the earth* (SFK)
Who put the colours in the rainbow? (JP) (CP)
Praise him (SG)
Fill your hearts with joy (CP)

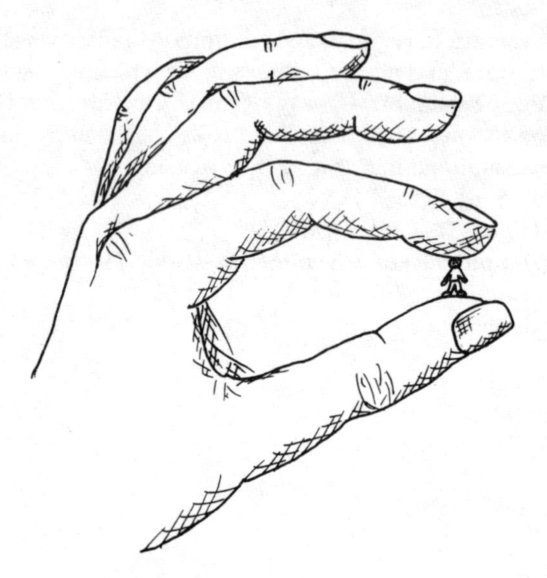

19. God Only Knows

Bible reference: Psalm 139

Teaching point: God knew us from the time we were conceived; he knows our thoughts, words and deeds

Equipment needed: A grain of rice

Take the grain of rice between your finger and thumb and show it at close range. Does anyone know what it is?

About three weeks after conception, each of us was the size of this grain of rice. No one could know anything about us.

Turn to Psalm 139:15. How fantastic God is! He knew all about me when I was this size! The whole psalm tells us how intimately God knows us. He knows our thoughts, words and deeds (verses 7–12).

It is pointless trying to hide our inner selves from God and keep any secrets. The only thing to do is what the psalmist did and invite God to have a good look!

Read the whole psalm together.

Songs: *I'm your child* (SFK)
Do not be afraid (SFK)
Whether you're one (JP)
There's no one in the world like Jesus (SG)
God knows me (CP) (JP) (SG)

20. *What a Memory!*

Bible reference: Luke 12:6

Teaching point: God knows every single person in the world by name

Equipment needed: Twenty common objects; a tray or an overhead projector

Display the objects on a tray or silhouetted on the OHP for one minute. Then cover them over and see how many the children can remember. Use pencil and paper with older children. Younger ones may call out. Have your own list to tick off the items as they are called out.

Talk about memory and how difficult it can be to remember the items.

Did the children know there are over five thousand million people in the world today? And God knows every single one of them by name. He even knows inside each heart! He never forgets one! What a memory God must have. How great and wonderful he is!

Luke 12:6 goes even further. God knows every single sparrow!

Songs: *I'm special* (SFK) (JP)
Jesus' love is very wonderful (SFK) (JP) (SG)
There are hundreds and thousands (JP) (SG) (CP)

21. *Allsorts—but No Favourites*

Bible reference: Acts 10:34

Teaching point: God has no favourites

Equipment needed: A box of liquorice allsorts or another assortment of sweets

Announce your intention to start your talk with a treat. Take the box of sweets around and offer one to each child.

After you have finished, comment on how choosy some of the children were, how they had their favourite flavour, and so on.

Sadly, we are not only like that with sweets—we can be like it with people too. We can have our favourites. Imagine what it would be like if God was like that. What if he took a dislike to me? How terrible!

It is so wonderful to know that God is not like that. We know that he loves each one of us totally and completely. He has no favourites. Use an example like Zacchaeus or Saul of Tarsus if desired.

Songs: *I'm accepted* (SFK)
God is good (SFK)
He's got the whole world (JP) (SG) (CP)

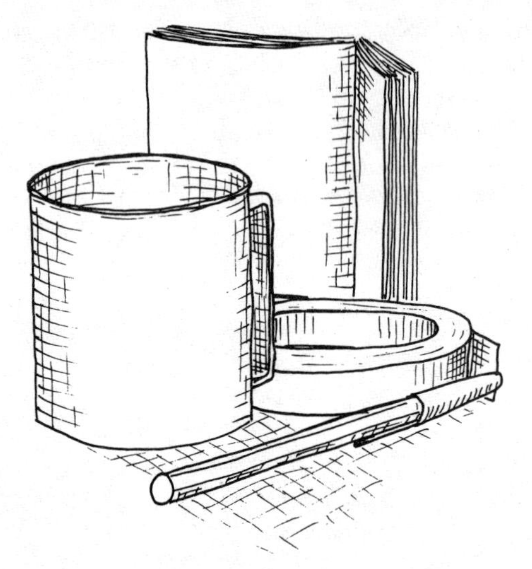

22. *Extra-ordinary*

Bible reference: 1 Corinthians 1:26–28

Teaching point: God's salvation is for very ordinary people

Equipment needed: A carrier bag full of 'ordinary' things, chosen because they have nothing significant or special about them; the above Bible verses inside a brown envelope at the bottom of the bag

Tell the youngsters you have brought along some things to show them. Pick up your bag and bring out the items one by one, with a commentary going something like this: 'Here I have a mug. Well, it's rather ordinary. There's nothing much I can say about it. What's next? Here is an exercise book. It's empty. Nothing special about it at all. Next comes a roll of sticky tape. Now why is that in the bag?' And so on until the bag is empty.

Only the envelope is left in the bag. Take it out and see what is in it. The Bible does say some amazing things! Read out the verses in the envelope.

God deliberately chose 'ordinary' people—people who have nothing special or significant about them at all. Does anyone present feel they are rather ordinary? Perhaps they never win at games, or shine in class. Perhaps they never come top or first. These are exactly the sort of people God wants to be his own! He deliberately chose each person present. We don't have to be rich, important or superstars to be special in God's eyes. He loves and wants ordinary people like you and me!

Songs: *Give thanks* (SFK)
I'm special (SFK) (JP)
It is a thing most wonderful (SG)
Song of Caedmon (CP)

23. *Start Counting . . .*

Bible reference: Luke 12:7

Teaching point: Those who confess Jesus as Lord are extremely important to God

Equipment needed: None

Get two volunteers who think they are good at counting to come forward. Tell them you have an extremely difficult task for them to do which even the cleverest mathematician in the world would not find easy. Ask one to count the hairs on the other's head.

Impossible? Perhaps if there is an adult present who is going bald, he or she would like to come forward and volunteer? Would that make it easier?

Still impossible? Jesus told his disciples something amazing about God. Look up Luke 12:7.

If God knows how many hairs we have on our heads, is there

anything he doesn't know? Apparently there are approximately 140,000 hairs on a dark-haired head, and approximately 80,000 on a blonde head. And God knows the exact number for every single person! Why did Jesus tell his disciples this incredible fact? To show them how important they were to God.

Songs: *O Lord, you're great* (SFK)
God who made the earth (JP) (SG) (CP)

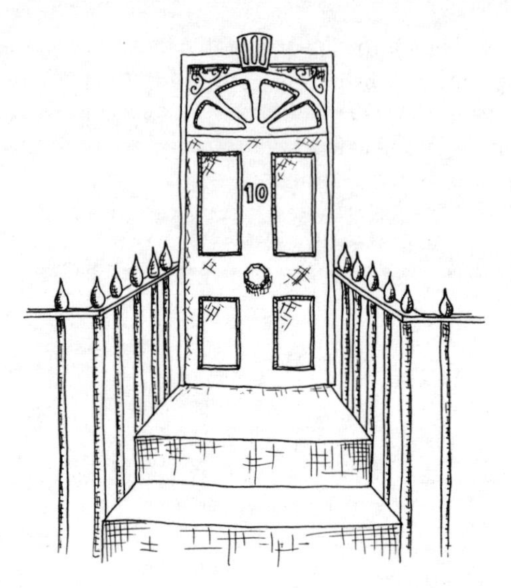

24. *And Now for the Good News*

Bible references: Isaiah 40:21–26; 41:4

Teaching point: God is in charge of history

Equipment needed: A list of well-known prime ministers, presidents, kings or queens; Bible verses written out on an OHP acetate or sheet of paper

Display Isaiah 40:21–26 and 41:4. The verses tell us that God is in charge of history.

Ask the following questions from the above passages (the answer is always 'the Lord'):

Who sits on his throne above the earth?

Who is so great that, compared to him, people seem like grasshoppers?

Who created the universe?
Who brings down princes and rulers?
Who is from the first to the last?
Who has a name for every star?
Who keeps the universe going?
Who makes plans and carries them out without fail?
Who is the greatest of all?

Follow on with 'Who is more powerful than . . . ?', running down your list of prime ministers, presidents, kings or queens. Have the children answer in unison: 'The Lord!'

When we watch the news on TV, we can sometimes think that the world is going out of control and feel scared. We need to remember that God is always in control.

Songs: *The earth is the Lord's* (SFK)
All over the world (SFK) (JP)
I do not know what lies ahead (JP)
Yesterday, today, for ever (SG) (JP)
Spirit of peace (CP)

25. *No News Is Good News*

Bible reference: Isaiah 40:9–11

Teaching point: God's good news rarely hits the headlines

Equipment needed: A recent newspaper for each pair of children

Give out a newspaper to each pair of children and ask them to find any 'good news'. Read out the appropriate headline and summarise the story. Good news can be difficult to find as often the news that is reported is not 'good news'.

Look together at Isaiah 40:9–11. These verses tell us that God wanted the people of Jerusalem to know the good news that God was coming. He told the messenger to go up on a high mountain and shout it out as he didn't want anyone to miss it!

This was a prophecy. It came true many years later when Jesus was born. His coming was God's coming. However, it was missed by the press as far as we know. The message of Jesus is still 'good news'—many miracles take place in people's lives, but it is almost impossible to read about them in the newspapers. All over the world today the church is growing as never before. The real news is not in the papers.

If desired, read out some facts and figures from Christian publications which highlight the amazing growth that is taking place in the Christian world, prefaced by the phrase 'Did you know. . .?'

Songs: *How lovely on the mountains* (SFK) (JP)
All over the world (SFK) (JP)
Hallelujah, for the Lord our God (JP)
There's no greater name than Jesus (SG)
O Lord, all the world belongs to you (CP)

26. *The Time of My Life*

Bible reference: Ecclesiastes 3:1–8

Teaching point: God has a right time for everything to happen

Equipment needed: An appointment diary or filofax

Show your diary or filofax and explain why and how you use it.

God has a diary for each one of us, but we cannot always look at it in advance! Look at Ecclesiastes 3:1–8 together. How many different times might there be in our lives? God has ordained every one of them for us. Whatever happens, we need never be afraid. God is in charge. He is with us.

Which of these 'times' do the youngsters feel is appropriate for them now?

Songs: *Be bold, be strong* (SFK) (JP)
Be thou strong (SG)
To everything turn (CP)

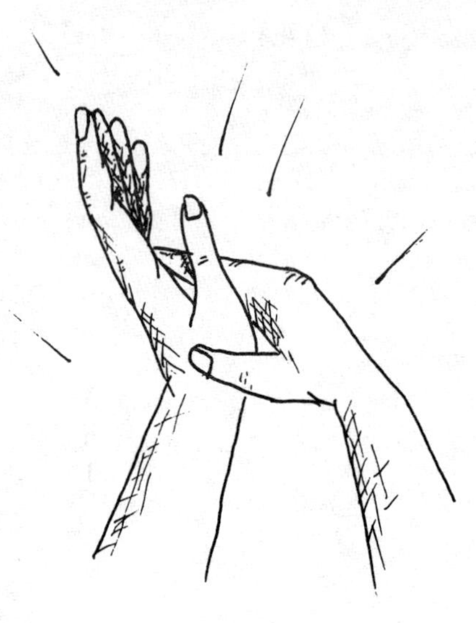

27. *Clap Your Hands*

Bible reference: Psalm 47

Teaching point: We can clap our hands with joy in worship to God

Equipment needed: The words of the song below written out on an OHP acetate or large sheet of paper

Sing the following song in a round using the well-known tune of Frère Jacques. Divide the children into four.

> Praise the Father, praise the Father,
> Praise the Son, praise the Son,
> Praise the Holy Spirit, praise the Holy Spirit,
> God is one, three in one.

Holy Father, holy Father,
Mighty Son, mighty Son,
Precious Holy Spirit, precious Holy Spirit,
God is one, three in one.

Look up Psalm 47:1. What does the psalmist tell all peoples to do? The rest of the psalm gives us reasons why we should clap our hands for joy. What are some of these reasons?

Try the round again, this time clapping out the rhythm instead of singing.

Choose one of the songs below, and during one verse invite people to stop singing and clap the rhythm—it's quite difficult! If you have a drummer, have him or her drum one verse while everyone listens.

Songs: *I will wave my hands* (SFK)
Can't stop my hands from clapping (SFK)
Clap your hands, all you people (JP)
Come and praise the Lord our King (SG)
You've got to move (CP)

28. *It's Quite OK to Shout*

Bible references:	Psalm 33:1–3; 47:5–9; 81:1
Teaching point:	We can praise God by shouting at the tops of our voices
Equipment needed:	A 'shoutometer'—ie, a piece of cardboard cut into a circle, with the numbers one to ten written around the circumference and an arrow attached to the centre with a paper fastener

Start by talking about shouting. Where and when do we shout? The school playground can be a very noisy place with high levels of excitement.

Show your home-made 'shoutometer'. This is to measure how loud a person can shout. Choose five or six volunteers and ask them to shout in turn: 'God is a great king.' As each one does so, give them a score on your 'shoutometer'.

Look at some of the above verses and conclude by shouting some of them together. Write some out on acetate if people have different Bible versions.

Songs: *It's amazin' what praisin' can do* (SFK)
Shout for joy and sing (SFK)
Live, live, live (JP)
What a wonderful Saviour is Jesus (SG) (SFK) (JP)
Praise the Lord in everything (CP)

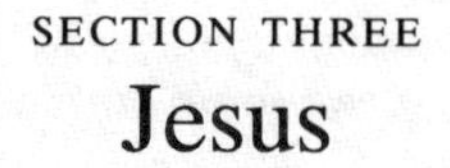

SECTION THREE

Jesus

29. He's the Image of His Father

Bible references: John 14:8–9; Colossians 1:15; Hebrews 1:3

Teaching point: Jesus, a human being, was God in action

Equipment needed: A large-ish mirror

Start by talking about how people want to 'see' God, and find it hard to believe in someone they cannot see. Perhaps some of the youngsters think it would be easier to believe in God if they could see him?

One of Jesus' disciples had this very problem. Philip said

to Jesus in John 14:8: 'Show us the Father, that is all we need.' Jesus' reply to Philip was staggering. He said: 'Whoever has seen me has seen the Father' (Jn 14:9).

Turn your back on the children and look in the mirror. Turn the mirror so that everyone is able to see your reflection.

Jesus was God's perfect reflection. If we want to see God clearly, we should read all about Jesus to get a complete picture.

Songs: *I believe in Jesus* (SFK)
God so loved the world (JP)
God is love (SG) (CP)

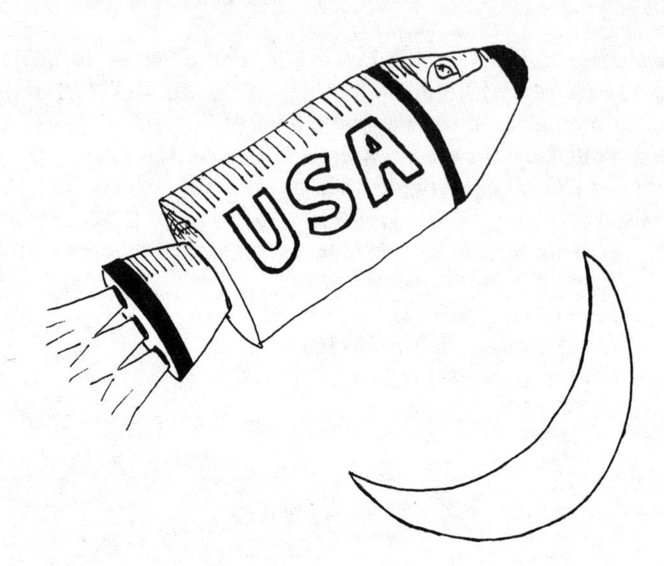

30. *One Way Only*

Bible reference: John 14:6

Teaching point: Jesus is the one way to know God personally

Equipment needed: (optional) an illustration of the moon; an illustration of a space rocket

Do any of the children know how far the moon is from the earth? (Answer: 238,860 miles.) Has anyone ever been to the moon? (Answer: in July 1969 the US spacecraft, Apollo 11, landed two men. A further five manned visits to the moon were made between 1969 and 1972.) Would any of the children like to visit the moon themselves? Could it be possible?

Does anybody sometimes feel that God is a long way away? Perhaps they know he is there, but feel he is unreachable. Perhaps they feel that only special people can be close to God, just as only a few selected people have visited the moon.

Is there a way to reach God? The way is open to absolutely everybody, and millions of people have discovered it. Jesus said: 'I am the way, the truth and the life. No one can come to the Father except by or through me.'

If we want to reach God, we have to put our faith and trust in Jesus. Anyone can do it!

Songs: *If you say Jesus is Lord* (SFK)
How I love you (SFK)
I am the way (JP) (SG)
When Jesus walked in Galilee (CP)

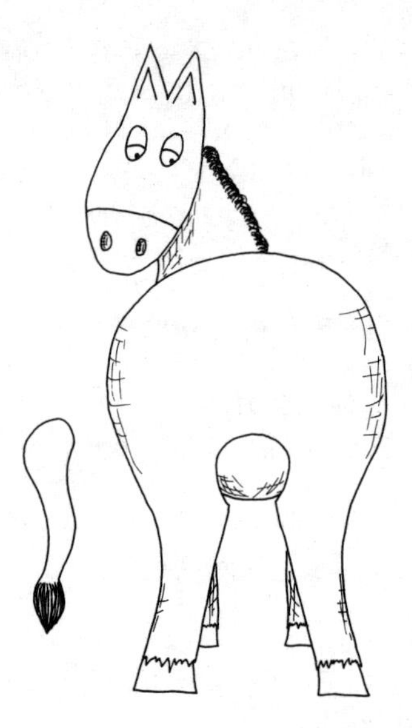

31. *The Light of the World*

Bible references: John 8:12; 1 John 1:5; Psalm 36:9; Ephesians 4:18; 2 Corinthians 4:4–6

Teaching point: For those who follow Jesus, it is as though they are living their lives in 'light'; for those who do not follow Jesus, it is as though they are living in 'darkness'

Equipment needed: A blindfold; a drawing of a donkey with a separate tail for a game of 'pin the tail on the donkey'

Play 'pin the tail on the donkey'. Blindfold volunteers and let them try to attach the donkey's tail to the correct part of its hind quarters. Then ask someone to do this without the blindfold.

Ask the question: 'Who said "I am the light of the world"?' Explore some of the meaning behind this statement. Obviously,

Jesus was not literally a source of light. What was he talking about? This was a very stupendous claim for Jesus to make. Only the Son of God could ever say such a thing.

The Bible tells us that those who do not believe in Jesus are wearing blindfolds—not the type of blindfolds that the volunteers wore earlier, but blindfolds inside their hearts and minds (Eph 4:18). We need to see what we are doing to put the donkey's tail in the right place. We need to see by the light of Jesus to live our lives in God's way. How awful to rely on guesswork to live the only life each one of us has!

However, with the light of Jesus shining in our hearts we know that we are living as God wants us to. We can 'see' where we are going. Use the Bible references to emphasise the point if desired.

Songs: *Lord, the light of your love* (SFK)
I have seen the golden sunshine (JP)
Keep me shining, Lord (SG)
From the darkness came light (CP)

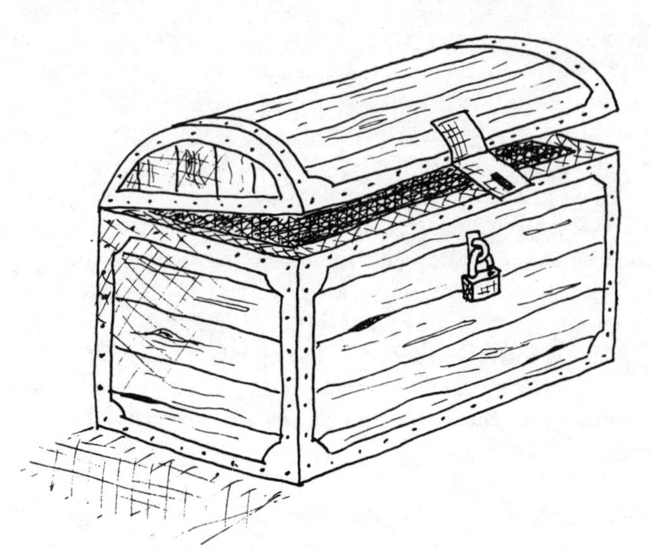

32. *Priceless!*

Bible reference: Matthew 13:44–46

Teaching point: Jesus is worth more than any fortune!

Equipment needed: One or two items which are of value to you—personal 'treasures'

Bring out your 'treasures' and explain why they mean so much to you. Have any of the youngsters got anything special which they treasure?

Jesus told two parables about treasure. Does anyone know what they were? Look at the above reference if necessary. What do these parables mean?

God's kingdom is the greatest treasure of all. Jesus is the greatest find of all. He is so valuable that all of our treasure becomes worthless in comparison. People who find Jesus give up everything else to follow him. When anyone finds him they find riches beyond compare.

Songs: *Lord, you are so precious* (SFK)
Lord, you are more precious (SFK)
Jesus, how lovely you are (JP) (SFK)
Sing his praises (SG)
Jesus Christ is here (CP)

33. *All Welcome!*

Bible references: John 6:37; Matthew 11:28

Teaching point: Jesus welcomes everyone who comes to him

Equipment needed: A large sheet of paper with a circle drawn on it

If this talk is being given in a church service, ask the children to approach everyone in the entire congregation, shake hands with them and say, 'Welcome.' They are to make sure no one is missed out.

Just as the children welcomed everyone, so Jesus welcomes everyone. There is no one who Jesus rejects; no one who is not welcome; no one he prefers not to speak to; no one he does not want a relationship with.

On a large piece of paper which has a circle drawn on it, ask everyone to come and draw a picture each of themselves or write their name in the circle during the singing of a song (depending on group size!).

Songs: *Lord, we've come to worship* (SFK)
It's me, O Lord (JP)
God is love, his the care (SG)
You can't stop the rain (CP)

34. *Children Are Special*

Bible reference: Mark 10:13–16

Teaching point: Jesus blesses children who are brought to him by faith, just as he blessed them in his lifetime

Equipment needed: None

If this talk is being given in a church service, ask the congregation to put up their hands if they went to Sunday school or Bible club regularly when they were children. Get some children to count the hands raised.

Then ask those who had no Christian teaching at all when they were young to raise their hands. Get some other children to count these.

Compare the two figures.

Read or tell the story of how Jesus blessed the children when they were brought to him (found in Mark 10). Notice how important Jesus thought these children were. Notice how he took them in his arms and blessed each individually. Ask the children to imagine what effect the direct blessing of Jesus might have had on these children's lives. We are not told who the children were or what happened to them afterwards. The story tells us that we do not have to wait until we are grown up to meet Jesus and receive his blessing.

The members of the congregation who raised their hands first have experienced blessing from Jesus himself as they came to learn about him when they were young.

It is very exciting for the children present because they are being blessed by Jesus now. He is present, not in person, but in the power of his Holy Spirit. He still loves children and wants to bless them. As the children come to the meeting they are coming to Jesus. Who knows what effect this will have on their future lives?

Songs: *You may think I'm so young* (SFK)
I'm your child (SFK)
Jesus is a friend of mine (JP)
Jesus' love is very wonderful (SG)(SFK)(JP)
Fill your hearts with joy (CP)

35. *I Feel Awful*

Bible reference: Mark 2:17

Teaching point: Jesus came to help those who are spiritually 'sick'

Equipment needed: Crutches (if available); sling; bandages; sticking plaster

Out of sight, get someone to help you dress up. Put a bandage round your head, a sticking plaster on your face, a bandage around one foot, your arm in the sling and make your entrance.

As you limp into position, complain about how your head hurts, your foot hurts, and you are bruised all over because you fell down the stairs. Unfortunately you are someone who cannot stand pain and you are suffering terribly!

Ask someone beforehand to interrupt you by reading out Mark 2:17. What was Jesus referring to when he said he had come for those who are 'sick'? Can someone explain exactly what he meant? Who are those who are 'sick'? How is Jesus a 'doctor'?

Take off your bandages as you explain that Jesus was using a picture to describe people who know they are sick and sinful in their hearts. He specifically came to bring forgiveness and wholeness to such people.

Finish your talk by asking the question: 'Who knows they need Jesus?' Be the first one to put up your hand. We all need the 'doctor' to heal our sinful hearts.

Songs: *Shout for joy and sing* (SFK)
You are my hiding place (SFK)
In my need, Jesus found me (JP)
Jesus is the name we worship (SG)
The King of love (CP) (JP)

36. *All Forgiven*

Bible references:	Romans 3:23–26; Luke 7:47
Teaching point:	Everyone needs to be forgiven by Jesus' death on the cross, whether their sins are few or many
Equipment needed:	An iron (with heavy duty extension lead if necessary); an ironing board; some very creased items to iron; some items which hardly need ironing

Make up a story to explain why you need to do some ironing (such as being behind with the chores) as you set up the ironing board and plug in the iron.

Show a very creased item of clothing to the children and as you iron it describe how it is becoming really smooth and wrinkle free. Show it proudly when it is finished. As you move to an uncreased item, point out that although it is not too bad it still wants an iron. Show this item when it is ironed. Continue with a similar running commentary as you iron a few more items.

Stop ironing, and from behind the ironing board explain how Jesus died on the cross to forgive our sins. Some people have done the most evil things in their lives and they badly need forgiveness. They are like the terribly screwed up clothes which badly need ironing. Other people are quite nice on the outside and perhaps seem quite good in lots of ways. They are like the clothes that are not in such need of the iron. Nevertheless, they all need ironing, and once they are ironed they are all the same: perfectly smooth and flat; completely forgiven. Whatever our condition, we must come to Jesus, humbly asking for his forgiveness and cleansing. He smoothes everybody out completely!

Whether we have lots of sins or few sins, we all need the forgiveness of Jesus.

Songs: *I get so excited, Lord* (SFK)
God forgave my sin (SFK) (JP)
To God be the glory (JP)
Living, he loved me (SG)
Our Father, who art in heaven (CP)

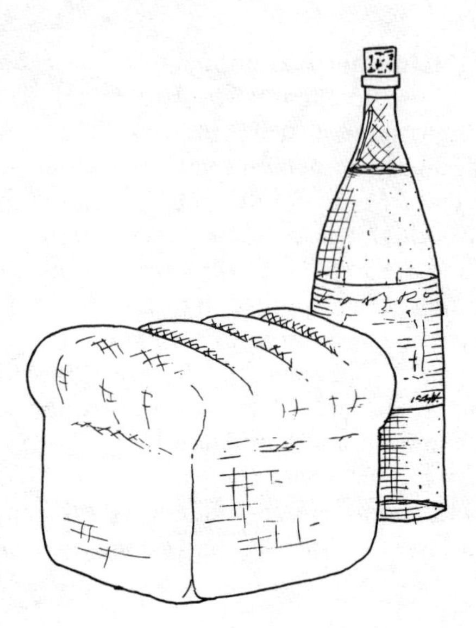

37. *Take It*

Bible reference: Mark 14:22–24

Teaching point: Jesus gave his life for us

Equipment needed: A valuable gift which you have been given; a loaf of bread; a jug of wine or juice

Begin by talking about your gift, explaining that you did nothing at all to deserve it—you did not have to pay for it, nor do anything in return.

Move on to talk about how Jesus gave something to his disciples before he died. Show the loaf of bread and the jug of wine. Jesus gave them to his disciples saying they represented something. Look up Mark 14:22–24.

Notice what Jesus said when he gave the disciples the bread and the wine. He said, 'Take it.' If he were here with bread and wine now, wouldn't he say to us, 'Take it,' just as he did to his disciples? Jesus is offering us today not just a piece of bread and a drink of wine, but what they represent: his life, given freely for us. We simply have to 'take it'.

Songs: *Grace is* (SFK)
Thank you for the cross (SFK)
It is a thing most wonderful (JP)(SG)
A man for all the people (CP)

38. *All Clean*

Bible references: Isaiah 1:18; Hebrews 10:10; Genesis 3

Teaching point: The blood of Jesus cleanses us from all sin

Equipment needed: A glass bowl full of water; red food colouring; bleach

Briefly tell the story of Genesis 3 (how sin entered the world), showing the clear bowl of water and staining it with food colouring as you do so. Once the water is red, there is no going back. Once sin had entered the world, every human being was affected. Add more food colouring as you say how the Bible tells us that the sins that men began to commit got worse and worse, until unimaginable evils were being committed.

God gave his laws to show people how to live in a good relationship with him and with each other, but man's wickedness spoiled that too.

Read Isaiah 1:18. Pour plenty of bleach into the bowl of red water and describe how Jesus took our sins upon his own body when he died on the cross.

Songs: *Thank you for the cross* (SFK)
He paid a debt (JP)
We want to tell you of Jesus' love (SG)
Peace, perfect peace (CP)

39. *The Work's Done*

Bible references: John 4:34; 19:28–30

Teaching point: Jesus completely finished the work of salvation when he died on the cross

Equipment needed: Items that are in the making but which are unfinished—eg, a picture being coloured in, an unfinished thank-you letter or a jumper partly knitted

Engage the children in conversation about starting things and not finishing them. Things like jigsaw puzzles, models and embroidery can be started with enthusiasm but discouragement can soon take over. Show your own unfinished items and make comments about them.

Jesus had an extremely difficult task to do when he lived on this earth. Read Hebrews 7:23–27. What a task! He was to be the one who would reconcile God and man by living a totally perfect life and then by offering himself as a sacrifice for our sins. But Jesus didn't give up. He finished the job. When he died on the cross he accomplished everything he set out to do.

Jesus did everything needed to make us completely acceptable to God. We didn't have to do the work ourselves. We can have confidence in his dying words: 'It is finished.' (The 'work' we have to do is to believe in Jesus, the Son of God—John 6:29.)

Songs: *Jesus, we celebrate your victory* (SFK)
Saviour of the world (JP)
Who took fish and bread (SG)(JP)
Come and praise (CP)

40. *In My Place He Stood*

Bible reference: John 18:39–40

Teaching point: Jesus died in my place

Equipment needed: Pairs of items such as: a penny and a £5 note; a small Lego toy and a large box of Lego; a small sweet and a box of chocolates; designer label trainers and ordinary trainers

Pretend that you have some difficult choices for the children to make. Reveal your pairs of items one by one and ask the children which item of each pair they would choose to have.

Barabbas was a murderer who was in prison when Jesus was arrested. If either Barabbas or Jesus could be set free, which one would the children choose?

This was the very choice that Pilate gave to the crowd who were waiting outside his palace in Jerusalem. Can you believe it?

They shouted for Barabbas, not Jesus. The result of this choice was that Jesus was crucified and Barabbas was set free.

Ask one of the children to come forward and imagine the same crowd choosing between him or her and Jesus. Which one would the crowd shout for? They were so determined that Jesus should die that they would have shouted for the child and Jesus would be the one to die. Whoever had been standing there would have been freed. Barabbas represents you and me.

This is the good news of the gospel of Jesus Christ. We live, because he died.

Songs: *Thank you, Jesus* (SFK)(JP)
You laid aside your majesty (SFK)
Barabbas was a bad man (JP)
Out there amongst the hills (SG)
As I went riding by (CP)

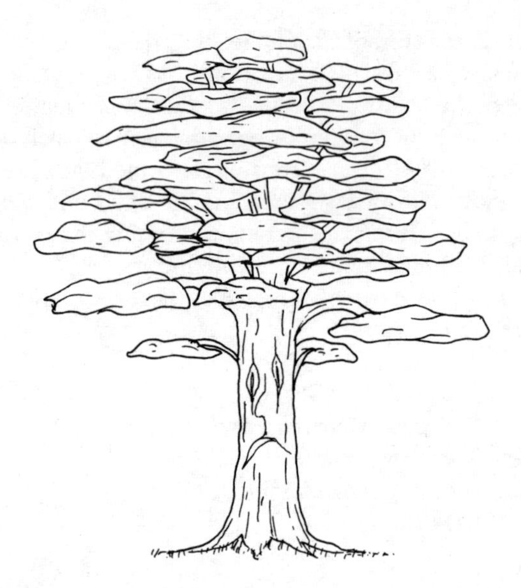

41. *Groan, Groan!*

Bible references: Romans 8:19, 22–23; Acts 1:11; 1 Thessalonians 4:16–17

Teaching point: The whole of creation is waiting with great anticipation for the return of Jesus

Equipment needed: None

Ask several volunteers to come out and stand in a straight line. Ask them one by one to 'groan'. As each one 'groans' express sympathy and comment on how convincing they sound. Perhaps the boys could all groan together? Can the girls make a louder and more desperate sounding groan? When might someone groan in real life?

The Bible tells us that the whole of nature is groaning all day and all night. Look together at Romans 8:19 and 22 and explain these verses.

Look up or tell of some of the details of the return of Jesus from heaven and how Christians will have new bodies and be gathered up in the air with Jesus. All of nature is groaning as it waits for this event!

Songs: *O, heaven is in my heart* (SFK)
When the trumpet of the Lord (JP)
When he comes (SG)
I've got peace like a river (CP)

SECTION FOUR

The Holy Spirit

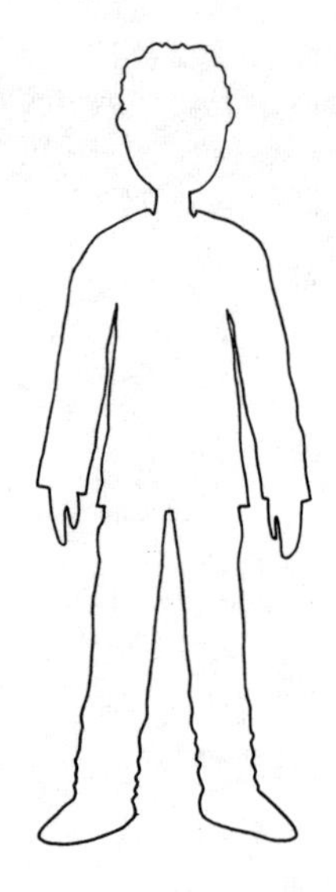

42. Just Like Jesus

Bible references: John 14:16; Acts 16:7

Teaching point: Jesus and the Holy Spirit have exactly the same nature

Equipment needed: An OHP acetate or blackboard on which is drawn the outline of a man

Ask the children to describe Jesus' character. What sort of person was he? Write their answers around the outline of the man. Answers will no doubt be words like: 'kind', 'loving', 'powerful' and 'holy'. Give hints and suggestions as necessary and build up as full a picture as possible.

Refer to John 14:16. Jesus says that he and the Holy Spirit are just the same (NB, the Greek word for 'another' means 'one who is identical'). When the Holy Spirit comes, it is just as though Jesus himself is with us. He will live in us, and he will remain with us for ever. If desired, in order to explain how the Holy Spirit took Jesus' place, tell the story of Jesus' ascension into heaven and the coming of the Holy Spirit.

Rub out your original outline and in the space left write the words: 'THE HOLY SPIRIT'. The Holy Spirit does not have a human body like Jesus had, but otherwise he is exactly the same as Jesus, and he will be with us for ever.

The Holy Spirit is the Spirit of Jesus. How wonderful! He comes to indwell those who put their faith in Jesus.

Songs: *Holy Spirit, fill me now* (SFK)
You are my God and Father (SFK)
He lives! (JP)
With the Father when the world began (SG)
Spirit of God (CP)

43. *Out of Breath?*

Bible reference:	Romans 8:1–8
Teaching point:	It is impossible to live the Christian life without the Holy Spirit within
Equipment needed:	None

Ask for two volunteers who are good at running to come forward. Ask them to see who can run on the spot for the longest time. Just as they are about to start, tell one volunteer he must hold his breath while he does it! Keep up a running commentary as they do this.

It is too hard to live the Christian life without the 'breath' of the Holy Spirit. We cannot keep it up over a long period of time. It takes a great effort, and we become discouraged and feel a sense of failure. It is like trying to run without breathing.

However, the Holy Spirit gives us the ability to live the Christian life naturally and to keep going!

Songs: *Not by might* (SFK)
When the Spirit of the Lord (SFK)
Love, joy, peace and patience (JP)
Spirit of God, unseen as the wind (SG)
You've got to move (CP)

44. *I'm a Plastic Cup*

Bible reference:	2 Corinthians 4:7
Teaching point:	God gives his wonderful treasure, the Holy Spirit, to ordinary human beings
Equipment needed:	A polystyrene or plastic cup; some good quality drink

Look together at the Bible verse, which will need explanation. What is the 'jar of clay' that Paul is talking about? What is the 'treasure'?

In the old days everyone drank from earthenware cups. Metal goblets were expensive. The ordinary beakers were made of clay and they were disposable. Today we use something else. Show the plastic cup. Clay jars or 'cups' were totally worthless and were thrown away just like our plastic cups. If Paul had been writing today he would have said: 'We have this treasure in plastic cups.'

Pour your drink into the plastic cup as you explain that we may be very ordinary people—frail and sinful, not rich or famous—but amazingly, God gives us himself in the person of the Holy Spirit. He comes and lives within us. God does not put his treasure into crystal glasses or silver goblets but into plastic cups!

Songs: *Rejoice, rejoice* (SFK)
Spirit of the living God (SFK)(JP)
With the Father when the world began (SG)
Spirit of God (CP)

45. *Candle Power*

Bible references: Acts 2:38–39; Luke 11:13; Matthew 5:14–16

Teaching point: The Holy Spirit is for every believer, without exception

Equipment needed: A selection of candlesticks varying in style, some ornate, some plain; some candles; matches

Show one of your candlesticks and ask if anyone knows what it is. Bring out a second one and point out all the differences between this one and the first. Continue in this way as you show your collection.

Despite the differences, these candlesticks have exactly the same purpose: to hold candles.

Just like these candlesticks, outwardly Christians can have few similarities. Mention some of the differences in your situation: old and young, boys and girls, etc.

Invite a youngster to come and light some candles. Meanwhile, explain that if Christians are like the candlesticks, then the Holy Spirit is like the candle. It is not the candlestick that gives light—it is the candle. The Holy Spirit inside us enables us to shine with the light of God. He can indwell every believer, whatever his or her shape and size.

Songs: *Light a flame* (SFK)
The promise of the Holy Spirit (SFK)
He lives (JP)
When God, the Holy Spirit (SG)
Spirit of peace (CP)

46. *Soaked Through for God*

Bible reference: Luke 5:1–11

Teaching point: It is important to be completely open to God and not try to keep him at arm's length

Equipment needed: An umbrella; a kagoule

Out of sight, put on the kagoule and put up the umbrella, then walk in to start your talk.

Ignore the fact that you are holding up an umbrella and talk quite normally. Begin to tell the children the story which is found in Luke 5 where Peter caught a great catch of fish.

Halfway through the story, ask if there is something wrong. You realise that you are wearing a raincoat and carrying an umbrella. Is there any reason why you are not free to do this if you wish? Carry on with the story.

When you have finished it, take your umbrella down and your

raincoat off. Say that it is possible for people to have invisible umbrellas up inside their hearts. The reason for this is that they do not want God to get too close to them. It is possible to say secretly to God, 'Depart from me,' just as Peter did. When Peter said this he was putting up his 'umbrella'. What was Jesus' response? He said, 'Don't be afraid.'

God sees right into our hearts. He knows we are sinful people. He wants to use us just like he used Peter. Jesus then said to Peter, 'From now on you will catch men.' God wants to fill us with his Holy Spirit, transform our dull occupations and use us to do all sorts of exciting things. For this to happen, though, we need to stop being afraid, take down our 'spiritual umbrellas' and welcome God by the power of his Holy Spirit into our lives.

Songs: *Sometimes it can be* (SFK)
Holy Spirit (SFK)
Spirit of the living God (JP)(SFK)
Come and serve the master (SG)
Spirit of God (CP)

47. *Keep Popping!*

Bible reference: 2 Corinthians 6:6–7; Acts 1:8

Teaching point: The Holy Spirit fills us with God's power

Equipment needed: A party popper

Show the party popper and ask the children what is packed away inside it. It is absolutely stuffed full with yards of thin tissue paper and a small amount of explosive. Talk about what it is used for and how it is quite useless as it is. All the potential inside has to be released.

God has given us the Holy Spirit. His power and life are packed inside us. However, we must not and cannot keep them in. The love, truth, faith and power that are inside us are to be released for the good of others. But, unlike the party popper, the more that we give out the more God refills us. Now, who wants to pop the popper?

Songs: *Here I am, Lord* (SFK)
Rejoice (SFK)
For I'm building a people of power (JP)
Holy Spirit came as fire (SG)
You've got to move (CP)

48. *Shine On!*

Bible reference: Acts 1:8

Teaching point: To teach that the Holy Spirit gives us power and makes us witnesses

Equipment needed: A torch with a separate battery

Show your torch and ask how many of the youngsters have their own torch. Tell a story involving torches from your own childhood, such as reading with a torch under the bedclothes or going on a midnight hike.

Switch on your torch and discover that it is not working. Let one or two youngsters examine the faulty torch. It will soon be noticed that it has no battery.

We are rather like the shell of a torch, and the Holy Spirit is like the battery. The Holy Spirit turns us into witnesses, just as a battery makes the torch light up. A torch can never work on its own, however hard it tries.

Look at Acts 1:8 together. Jesus promises that two things will happen when the Holy Spirit is given. The first is that we will receive power. The second is that we will be witnesses. When the Holy Spirit comes to dwell inside us we receive a power which we could not possibly have otherwise, and as a result we become witnesses. We will shine for Jesus.

Songs: *Lord, the light of your love* (SFK)
I am a lighthouse (SFK)(JP)
Wherever I am I will praise you, Lord (JP)
Holy Spirit came as fire (SG)
Every word comes alive (CP)

49. *Super-sensitive*

Bible references: John 16:8; Psalm 51:3–5; 1 John 1:8–9

Teaching point: Christians are sensitive to sin because of the presence of the Holy Spirit inside them

Equipment needed: A pile of cushions on the floor, with a dried pea hidden underneath them

Get some volunteers to sit on the cushions and see if they can guess what is hidden underneath.

Does anyone know the fairy-tale of the princess and the pea? Because she was a princess she could feel a single pea under her mattress when she slept. It is a very silly story because although our skin is very sensitive, it could never be sensitive enough to feel a pea under a mattress.

We are like princes and princesses because we are children of the King! One of the things the Holy Spirit does is to make us extra-sensitive—not to peas, but to sins like jealousy and lying, selfishness and sulkiness. We should not be surprised that we notice these 'peas' in our lives, because God wants us to admit that they are there and get rid of them. We can only get rid of them when we recognise them. Without the Holy Spirit, we do not even notice them. This sensitivity is an essential part of the Holy Spirit's work to make us like Jesus.

Songs: *Soften my heart* (SFK)
Let God speak (SFK)
I want to walk with Jesus Christ (JP)
Cleanse me (SG)(JP)
Spirit of God (CP)

50. *What a Load of Rubbish!*

Bible references: Galatians 5:22–23; 2 Corinthians 3:18

Teaching point: The Holy Spirit works in a believer's life to produce a wonderful character

Equipment needed: Some vegetable peelings; some garden or potting compost

Ask some questions and talk about compost heaps. What is a compost heap? Who has one in his or her garden or knows someone who has? What is put on it? What is it for?

Show your vegetable peelings. When these are put outside in a big pile with other garden rubbish—like weeds, tea-bags, grass or egg-shells—and left for a few months, they undergo an amazing transformation. The action of minute bacteria and worms changes the peelings into an excellent fertiliser. Show your compost.

A similar miracle takes place in the lives of Christians. The Holy Spirit works inside us to make us into wonderful people. Use Galatians 5:22–23, and, holding the vegetable peelings in one hand and the compost in the other, list the fruits of the Spirit and their opposites. The Holy Spirit changes our impatience into patience, our unbelief into faith, our despair into hope, and so on.

Develop the idea as required. We cannot change ourselves—only the Holy Spirit has the power to change us. We need to be 'on the compost heap'—in the fellowship of the church—for any change to take place. Any old peelings can be changed from useless rubbish to useful soil. God can take any life, change it and use it to his glory.

Songs: *Here I am, Lord* (SFK)
Change my heart, O God (SFK)
Love, joy, peace and patience (JP)
Like Jesus (SG)
Heavenly Father, may thy blessing (SG)(CP)

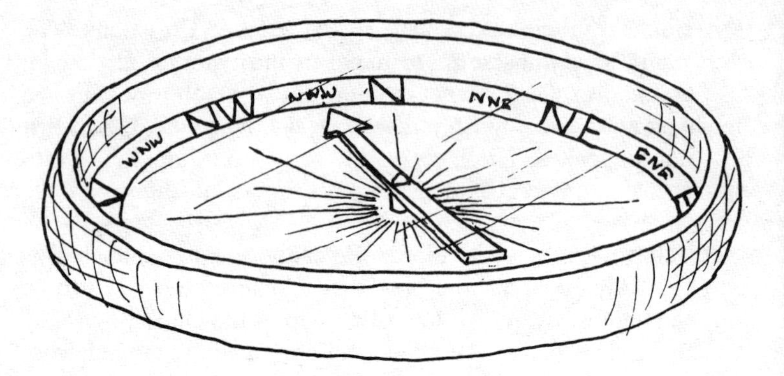

51. Which Way?

Bible references: Isaiah 30:21; John 16:13–14

Teaching point: The Holy Spirit is our guide

Equipment needed: A compass

Ask the children to point to north at a given signal. Check who is right with the compass. Then try to confuse the youngsters by turning round, going to a corner or standing on a chair and asking where north is from those positions.

Whatever position we are in, a compass will direct us accurately to north. The Holy Spirit is our inner 'guide'. Look up John 16:13–14. The Holy Spirit will keep us on the right path, always pointing us to Jesus.

Songs: *We are marching* (SFK)
Father, I place into your hands (SFK)(JP)
I do not know what lies ahead (JP)
We are marching home (SG)
One more step (CP)

SECTION FIVE

The Bible

52. *Both Needed*

Bible references:	Isaiah 59:21; 2 Peter 1:20
Teaching point:	The Holy Spirit and the Bible together are essential in our Christian lives
Equipment needed:	A padlock and a key that turns it; a tin of food and a tin opener; a nut and some nut-crackers

Begin by showing the lock and asking what it can be used for. After receiving a few suggestions, begin to question whether they are correct. After all, a lock has no single use at all without a key. Make exactly the same point using the can and the nut.

We need the Holy Spirit to help us read and understand the Bible. Otherwise the Bible is just an academic book. It has no life. It is like a padlock with no key. Also, the Holy Spirit on his own without the Bible is like the key with no padlock, or the tin opener with no tin. The Holy Spirit confirms God's written word. God has given the two together, and only when they are working together do we have everything we need for our Christian lives. Let us be both students of God's word and filled with the Holy Spirit.

Songs: *We believe* (SFK)
Make the book live to me (JP)(SG)
Spirit of peace (CP)

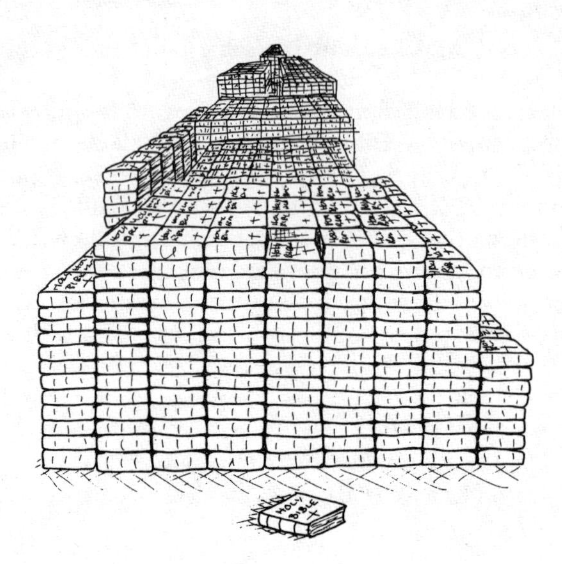

53. *Best Seller*

Bible reference: 2 Timothy 3:16

Teaching point: Belief in the Bible as the inspired word of God is not at all irrational

Equipment needed: A large notice with the words 'The Bible' written on it

Begin a series of questions which point out what a unique historical document the Bible is. The answer to each question is 'the Bible', so choose a volunteer to hold up the answer card after each question. Here are some examples to which you can add facts of your own:

Which book is the world's best seller?

Which book has thirty million copies printed and distributed each year?

Which book has been translated into 1,200 or more languages?

Which is the only book that says over 4,000 times, 'This is what the Lord says'?

Old manuscripts of which book can sell for half a million pounds?

Which book has hundreds of prophecies which have come to pass?

Which is the only book which foretold the birth, death and resurrection of Jesus?

Which is the only book that has foretold the rebirth of an old nation—Israel?

Which book took over 1,600 years to finish?

Which book was written by over forty writers from three continents over 1,600 years—all of them agreeing with each other?

Which is the only book that has had thousands of other books written about it?

Which old book has thousands of old manuscripts (hand written copies) with very few discrepancies?

Which book can you read over and over again and keep finding something new?

Are we mad to believe the Bible is God's word? *No*!

(Facts from: Weiss, G. Christian, *The Bible*, Back to the Bible Publishers: Nebraska, USA, 1962.)

Songs: *Come on, let's go exploring* (SFK)
The best book to read (JP)(SG)
Fill your hearts with joy (CP)

54. *Guaranteed to Last*

Bible references:	Mark 13:1–2; 13:31; Isaiah 40:8
Teaching point:	Everything will come to an end sooner or later, but God's word will last for ever
Equipment needed:	None

Choose a well-known magnificent building near to you (it could be the church you are in!) and discuss its grandeur and architecture.

Jesus' disciples came from Galilee, which was some way from Jerusalem. They would not have been very accustomed to city life and to seeing grandiose buildings. What did one of them say to Jesus in Mark 13:1–2?

This disciple was obviously impressed by the magnificence of the temple. Was Jesus impressed? What did he say would happen? Approximately forty years after his death the words he spoke came true. The temple was totally destroyed by the Roman armies.

In Mark 13:31, Jesus said his words would last for ever. Isaiah 40:8 says that the word of God will last for ever. The building you have chosen will some day be gone, but the words of the Bible will last for ever. How amazing!

Songs: *O, heaven is in my heart* (SFK)
Yesterday, today, for ever (JP)(SG)
I've got peace like a river (CP)

55. *Food for Thought!*

Bible references: Ezekiel 3:1–2; Revelation 10:9–10

Teaching point: The Bible should not only inform our minds but should also affect the whole of our being

Equipment needed: A packet of 'roll out' cake icing (or rice-paper); some food colouring.

(NB This talk needs preparation at least one day before.)

Roll out the icing (which acts like Plasticine) to a rectangle about six inches by four, and about one quarter to half an inch thick. Shape it to make it look like a book. When it has hardened, paint the words 'The Bible' or 'God's Word' on the front with food colouring. Or use rice-paper to achieve the same end. Transport it carefully!

Start by talking generally about how important the Bible is. Proudly produce your new Bible. Then amaze everyone by starting to eat it. (It will certainly be as sweet as honey in your mouth!)

Protest that what you are doing is not unusual as two people in the Bible were told to do the very same thing. Get volunteers to look up the two references.

Ask the youngsters why they think John and Ezekiel were told to eat God's word as though it were food.

Usually we take in God's word through our minds, but it does us no good if it just stays in our brains as so much 'Bible knowledge'. God wants us to 'feed' on his word so that it affects all of our being. The Bible must affect our feelings, our words and our actions as well as our minds—just as the food we eat permeates our whole bodies and gives us the energy we need.

Songs: *Have you got an appetite?* (SFK)
I'm gonna say my prayers (SFK)
He brought me to his banqueting house (JP)
Make the book live to me (SG)
Fill thou my life (CP)

56. *Stick to the Recipe!*

Bible reference: 2 Timothy 3:16–17

Teaching point: The Bible has been given to us so that we may live our lives according to God's plans

Equipment needed: An apron; mixing bowl; wooden spoon; a Victoria sponge recipe; ingredients, including jam, sugar and salt

Put on the apron, take the wooden spoon and announce your intention to make a Victoria sponge.

Read out the recipe one stage at a time and follow the instructions, letting everyone see what you are doing. Make deliberate mistakes, such as adding wrong amounts and substituting one ingredient for another. For example, use jam instead of eggs, or salt instead of flour. As you mix it all together, say how much you love sponge cake and are looking forward to this one.

Show it to the children and encourage a reaction such as 'Ugh!' If desired, produce a sponge cake at this moment and say, 'Here is one I made earlier!'

Take off your apron and emphasise the point that when we are making cakes we know we have to follow the recipe carefully or the cake will taste awful. God has given us a recipe, not for cakes, but for our lives. Hold up a Bible. Sadly, many people ignore what God says and think that they can believe and do as they wish. They make up their recipe as they go along. God says in his word that this road leads to disaster.

Some people are such good cooks that they know the recipe off by heart. Let's get to know the Bible better so that we can follow God's guidelines really well.

Songs: *Father, your word* (SFK)
Have you got an appetite? (SFK)
I have decided to follow Jesus (SFK)(JP)
O Jesus, I have promised (SG)
Lead me from death to life (CP)

57. *An Atlas of God*

(First in a series of three talks on the Bible)

Bible reference:	2 Timothy 3:16
Teaching point:	The Bible is the place to look if we want to know about God
Equipment needed:	An atlas

Show your atlas and engage the children in conversation about its nature and purpose. We cannot see very far with our eyes. An atlas gives us a 'distance shot'.

If we want to know what God is like, what book do we use? Again, looking around us will not tell us much. The Bible gives us a grand overview, rather like an atlas. It tells us how magnificent God is and what sort of character he has. It tells us how he created the world and how he made men and women. It tells us he is in charge of the whole of history and has great plans for the future.

If we want to be informed about the geography of the world, we look at an atlas. If we want to know about the character of God and his purposes for the world, we read the Bible.

Songs: *Come on, let's go exploring* (SFK)
Make the book live to me (JP)(SG)
The Bible tells us of God's great plan (SG)
Fill thou my life (CP)

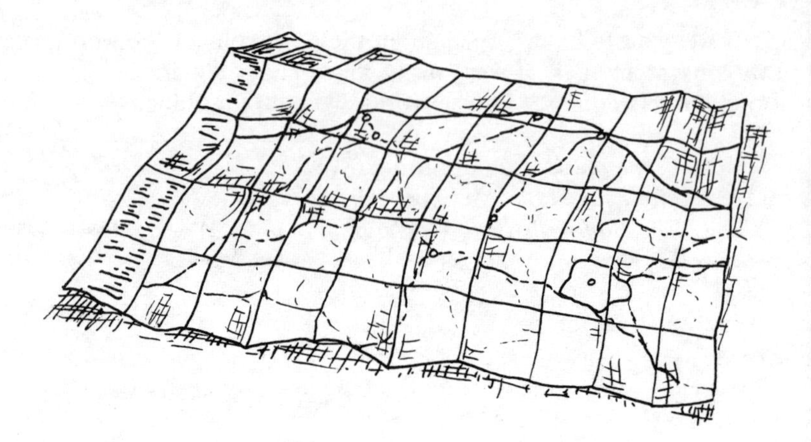

58. *Getting to Know Him*

Bible references: 2 Timothy 3:16; Matthew 7:24–27

Teaching point: The Bible is the book we need to read if we want to know God personally

Equipment needed: An atlas; a road map of the British Isles

Look at the atlas used in the last talk and try to find a page where you can discover how to get from your town or village to London or another large town. Begin to look frustrated and engage the children in the problem you have. Obviously, in this case the atlas is not the sort of map you need. Take the road map, turn to the right page and briefly chart your journey.

If we want to know the right way to live our individual lives, we need to look at the Bible where God has given his laws and plans for life. In it he tells all mankind how to get to know him and live their lives with Jesus as their Lord and Saviour.

Using the Bible can really help us get somewhere! Getting to know God is a bit like a journey, and to find the way effectively we need to study God's road map: the Bible.

Songs: *I have hidden your word* (SFK)
I am so glad (JP)(SG)
Fill your hearts with joy (CP)

59. *Right Down to the Last Detail*

Bible reference: 2 Timothy 3:16

Teaching point: The Bible directs us in the tiny details of our lives

Equipment needed: An atlas; a road map; a town map

Pretend you have been invited to someone's house which is in a small road in your town. You do not know exactly where it is. Look first at your atlas and then at your road map. These will not help you. What should you do?

If we want to find out where a particular street is in our town we need a map with an even smaller scale: a street map, or an Ordnance Survey map. These maps give details right down to houses, churches and parks.

The Bible is such a wonderful book. It tells me all I need to know about my life in its detail. It applies to each one of us as individuals every day.

Engage the children in describing how the Bible can apply to everyday life. There is nothing in our lives too small for God to be interested in. The Bible tells us what to do if we are afraid or confused. It tells us we can pray to God at any time. It tells us we can trust God in every circumstance. It tells us God is always with us.

The Bible is such an important book. It is our most valuable reference book. God has packed everything into one amazing book!

Songs: *You are my hiding place* (SFK)
God is our guide (JP)
For your holy book, we thank you (SG)
God, who made the earth (CP)

SECTION SIX

The Church

60. *God's Amazing Jigsaw*

Bible references: 1 Corinthians 12:12; Revelation 7:9

Teaching point: Jesus is building his church

Equipment needed: An overhead projector; a large-piece jigsaw with very few pieces; a jigsaw with hundreds of pieces. (The pictures on these puzzles do not matter.)

Arrange the pieces of the large-piece jigsaw at random on top of the overhead projector. Ask for a volunteer to come and assemble it. The pieces will show up in silhouette as it is assembled, as will the hands. As this is happening, use the jigsaw to illustrate how Jesus is fitting the people in your church together, and how each individual member is joined to all the others in love and unity. Each person, whether he or she is younger or older, has an essential part to play. Use examples from your own situation to illustrate how important everyone is.

When this puzzle is finished, remove it and pour the pieces of the other puzzle onto the projector. All the pieces are so small—this puzzle will take ages to do. This is like the worldwide church that Jesus is building. It has countless millions of members, and in this church too each one has a vital part.

Read out Revelation 7:9.

Songs: *We are one, we are family* (SFK)
For I'm building a people of power (JP)
Lift high the cross (SG)
Spirit of peace (CP)

61. Will the Real Church Please Stand Up?

Bible references: Matthew 16:18; Philemon 1–2; 1 Peter 2:5,9

Teaching point: 'Church' means people, not buildings

Equipment needed: None

Play a game of 'Simon says' using the name of your church with each instruction. For example:

Simon says: St Peter's Church, stand up.
Simon says: St Peter's Church, wave your arms in the air.
Simon says: St Peter's Church, jump up and down.
Sit down.
Simon says: St Peter's Church, sit down.

Then continue in this way:

Simon says: St Peter's Church, look up Matthew 16:18.
Simon says: St Peter's Church, read out Matthew 16:18.
Simon says: Jesus' building, stand up.
Simon says: St Peter's Church, look up Philemon 1–2.
Simon says: St Peter's Church, read out Philemon 1–2.
The church that meets at Philemon's house, sit down.
Simon says: The church that meets at St Peter's, sit down.

The church is the people and can meet anywhere. There is nothing sacred about buildings. It is the people who are important.

Songs: *I will build my church* (SFK)
We really want to thank you, Lord (SFK)(JP)
Long ago the friends of Jesus (SG)
Song of Caedmon (CP)

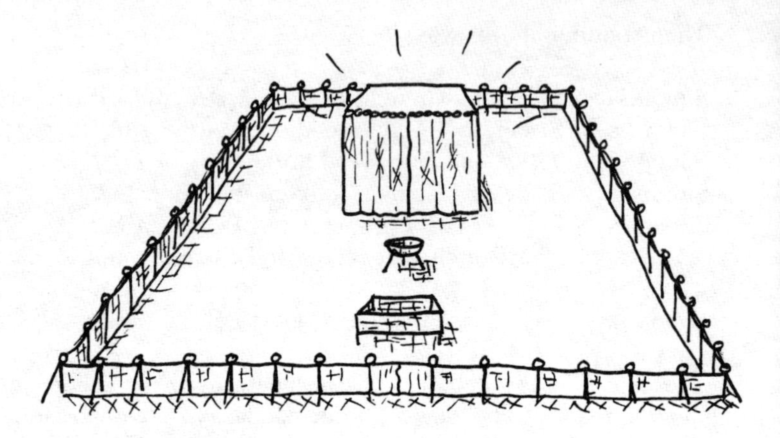

62. *Home Is . . . (1)*

Bible references: Exodus 25:8; 40:33–34

Teaching point: God wants to make his home with people and live in harmony with them

Equipment needed: A long piece of string; a sheet; Bible passages on OHP acetate (optional); diagram of tabernacle on OHP acetate (optional)

Make an instant tent by asking two volunteers to hold the string taut, draping the sheet over it and asking four more volunteers to hold down the corners. Can anyone imagine God living in a tent? He did! The people of Israel were living in tents and God wanted to live among them, so he lived in one as well.

Put Exodus 25:8 on the overhead projector and get everyone to read it together. Where did God want to live? Among the people!

Explain that God gave Moses careful instructions as to how to build a special tent for him because God wanted his new home to be like the one he has in heaven. (A photocopied or drawn OHP acetate of the tabernacle would be useful at this point.) God wanted his own special things in the tent, like a candlestick and an altar. Everything is explained in the book of Exodus.

Next put Exodus 40:33b–34 on the overhead projector and read it together. What happened when Moses had followed all of God's instructions and finished making the tent? God's presence came and filled it. He was really there, right in the middle of his chosen people!

Songs: *God is here, God is present* (SFK)
God is working his purpose out (JP)
God is good, we come before him (SG)
Rejoice in the Lord always (CP)

63. *Home Is . . . (2)*

Bible references: 1 Kings 6:1; 8:10-11

Teaching point: Solomon built a temple in Jerusalem and this became God's new dwelling place on earth

Equipment needed: A model of a temple made with small interlocking bricks (or a pile of bricks so that one or two youngsters can make one); Bible passages on OHP acetate (optional)

Produce your model, or if time permits, ask one or two youngsters to make a model of a temple. (This could happen during the singing of a song or some other item.)

Recap the previous talk. Tell the youngsters how God had promised the people of Israel a country where they could settle. Eventually, they moved into Canaan.

Put 1 Kings 6:1 up on the overhead projector and read it together. Explain how the people still had some of the furniture but the special tent itself had worn out after 480 years. The temple Solomon built was similar in design to the tent. We read all about it in 1 Kings 6–8.

Put 1 Kings 8:10-11 on the overhead projector and read this verse together. How amazing! Just as God's presence had filled the tent, so God's presence filled the temple! King Solomon knew that the whole universe was too small to contain God. But God really did want to live among his people and he moved straight in to his new home.

Songs: *Glory* (SFK)
Your ways are higher than mine (JP)
Open my eyes (SG)
Praise him (CP)

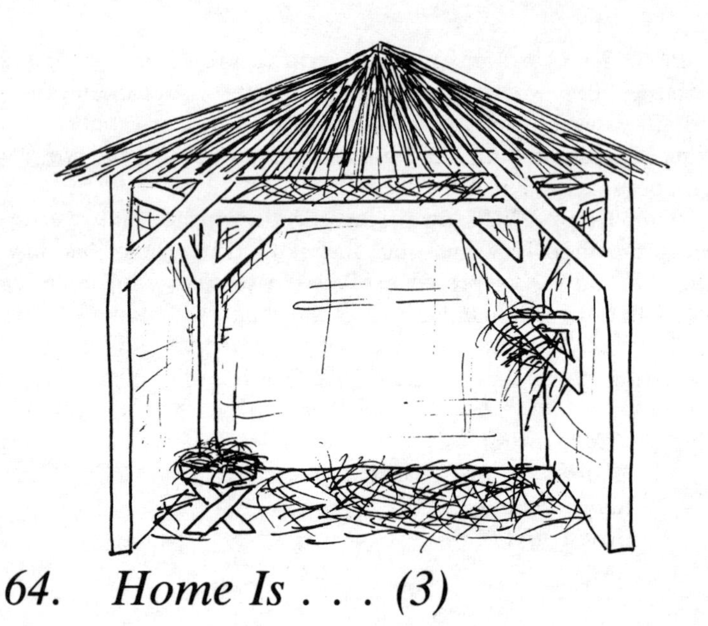

64. *Home Is . . . (3)*

Bible references: Matthew 1:23; John 2:21; Matthew 17:2

Teaching point: Jesus was 'God living among us' when he was alive on earth

Equipment needed: Bedroom slippers; a comfortable chair or bean-bag; a newspaper or book

Assemble the items in front of the youngsters, sit in the chair in a relaxed way, put on the slippers and pick up the book. Talk about how comfortable you are, how warm the slippers are and how at home you feel.

Describe how God's people began to forget about God as the years went by. Foreigners moved into the country and destroyed Solomon's wonderful temple. God still wanted to live with mankind, however, so he decided to do something very special indeed. He made himself at home with mankind by coming to live with them himself!

Read Matthew 1:23 together from the overhead projector. God was now with us, not in a tent or temple, but in a person—as a tiny baby to start with! Then read Matthew 17:2 together. The dazzling presence of God shone in Jesus on just this one occasion. Only three disciples saw it.

The Bible clearly teaches that Jesus was God himself. God was born as a baby and lived among people for thirty-three years. Jesus described himself as God's temple, God's dwelling place (Jn 2:21).

Songs: *Jesus, name above all names* (SFK)(JP)
He's great, he's God (JP)
No, never alone (SG)
Come and praise the Lord our King (CP)

65. Home Is . . . (4)

Bible references: Acts 2:2–4; Ephesians 2:22; Matthew 18:20; 1 Corinthians 3:16

Teaching point: God's dwelling place on earth is his church

Equipment needed: A large blank sheet of paper

Hold up the blank sheet of paper and pretend that it has a picture of a magnificent house upon it. Describe the gardens, the swimming pool, the wide front door. Interrupt your description by asking, 'Can't you see it?' When the response comes back, 'No!', put it down in exasperation saying you will come back to it later.

Recap the previous talks. Explain how Jesus returned to heaven when his ministry on earth was completed. But God did not want to stop living with mankind. Far from it! He wanted to live with more people than ever!

Read Acts 2:2–3 together. God's presence came down once again, not to fill a tent or a temple, but to fill the disciples as a group! The Holy Spirit is ready to fill anyone who believes in Jesus and repents of their sin. God's dwelling place on earth is now with believers of all nations—his church.

Read or display Ephesians 2:22 to emphasise the point.

Show the paper again. God's house has no walls, no garden, no swimming pool. But it is magnificent! We are God's house!

Finally, get everyone to write their name or draw a picture of themselves on the paper if appropriate.

Songs: *O, heaven is in my heart* (SFK)
I will build my church (SFK)
Live, live, live (JP)
He lives (SG)
Spirit of peace (CP)

66. *What an Assortment!*

Bible references: 1 Corinthians 12:5–6, 27–30; 1 Peter 4:10

Teaching point: Everyone has a different part to play in the church

Equipment needed: A selection of kitchen utensils, including some unusual ones

Go through the selection of utensils, seeing if the children know what each one is used for.

All these tools are for different tasks, and yet all are for use in the kitchen. Human beings like to have exactly the right tool for each different job and are very creative at getting each one exactly right.

Now, God is very creative too. He has created each one of us with many different uses and purposes, but with one main purpose: to glorify him. Give examples from the above references, or describe some of the people with their different roles in your own situation.

Songs: *Lord, we've come to worship you* (SFK)
Jesus, you love me (SFK)
Make me a channel of your peace (SFK)(JP)(CP)
Who can? What can? (SG)

67. *What a Row!*

Bible references: Psalm 133; John 17:11, 20-23

Teaching point: God wants his people to work and live together in harmony

Equipment needed: A selection of percussion instruments, like a triangle, maraca, drum—whatever you have

Ask for volunteers (not too young!) to come forward to play the instruments. When you say 'play' or 'go', ask them all to play together while you count to ten, then stop.

Was that a nice sound? How could it be improved? Get some suggestions from the children. They could play in turn, or keep to the rhythm of one tune. Get them to play together again, putting one of the suggestions into practice. Hopefully, there is a huge improvement. Try out one or two more of their suggestions and see which one sounded best.

(Alternatively, if you have a number of musicians present, arrange with them beforehand to have each play a different song simultaneously at a pre-arranged signal. Talk about how awful it sounded, and ask if anyone recognised what was being played. Then select just one of the songs and ask the group to play it together.)

Then ask someone to read Psalm 133 or John 17:21, and explain the verses in your own words.

The awful sound which was produced earlier was because everyone involved was 'doing their own thing' without any consideration for anyone else. It is quite possible to live out our lives like this—just doing what we want all the time. God hates this kind of selfishness. He wants us to co-operate with and care for each other.

Songs: *Jesus put this song* (SFK)
We will praise (SFK)
Bind us together (JP)(SFK)
Let us praise God together (SG)
Down by the riverside (CP)

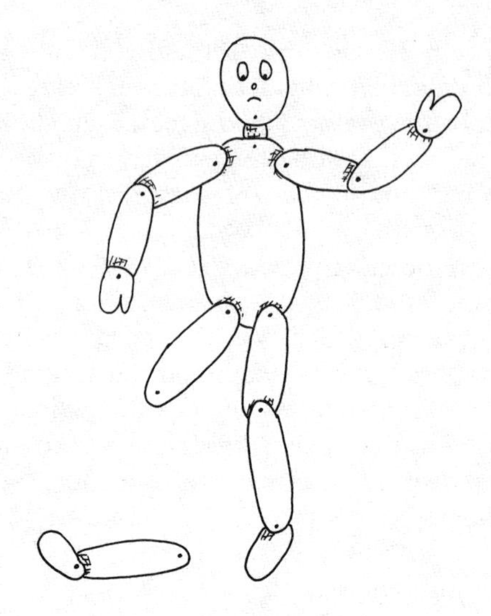

68. *Body Language*

Bible reference:	1 Corinthians 12:12–31
Teaching point:	The local church can be likened to a human body
Equipment needed:	Paper fasteners; a cardboard cut-out of different body parts: two legs, two feet, two arms, two hands, a trunk and a head, with holes in position so that the paper fasteners will hold them together when necessary

Show the children the parts of the body one by one, making comments on their shapeliness and usefulness.

The Corinthian church was described by Paul as being like these body parts. Read some verses from 1 Corinthians 12 to illustrate this point.

As Christians we are just as ridiculous on our own as these

body parts are. We belong together. We have the same blood running through our veins—the Holy Spirit (v13). We can be very different—different races, different characters, old or young (v13)—but we are like one body. We have different parts to play. We complement and serve one another. The mouth could not eat without the hands, and so on.

We must join the body together. There is no other way. Ask a volunteer to assemble the body parts with the paper fasteners.

Have everyone link arms or hold hands and sing one of the songs, perhaps walking around the room together.

Songs: *A new commandment* (SFK)
Encourage one another (SFK)
We really want to thank you, Lord (JP)(SFK)
Here we come with gladness (SG)
Love will never come to an end (CP)

69. *Opposition*

Bible references: Acts 5:17–21; 1 Peter 4:12–16; Hebrews 13:3

Teaching point: People who follow Jesus may get opposition and persecution

Equipment needed: Some pieces of cardboard about eighteen inches square, cut to look like prison bars

You need some volunteers willing to be sent to prison. Assemble as many as you have prison bars, less one, in a line at the front.

Ask the others what offence someone might have committed to warrant a prison sentence. As soon as a serious criminal offence is called out, send the first volunteer to prison by giving him a cardboard square to hold in front of his face. Continue asking for different offences until all the volunteers are 'in prison'.

You have one square left. Hold it up and read or tell the story from Acts 5. Is there another reason that someone might be sent to prison? Look up 1 Peter 4:12–16.

In many countries of the world today it is a criminal offence to be a Christian, just as it was in the days of the apostles. However, 1 Peter 4:12–16 tells us that it is an honour to suffer for Jesus.

If desired, mention a country where Christians are suffering for their faith, then pray for them together, reading Hebrews 13:3.

Songs: *The Lord will rescue me* (SFK)
Sometimes it can be (SFK)
Stand up, stand up for Jesus (JP)
There's a fight to be fought (SG)
One more step (CP)

SECTION SEVEN

The Christian Life

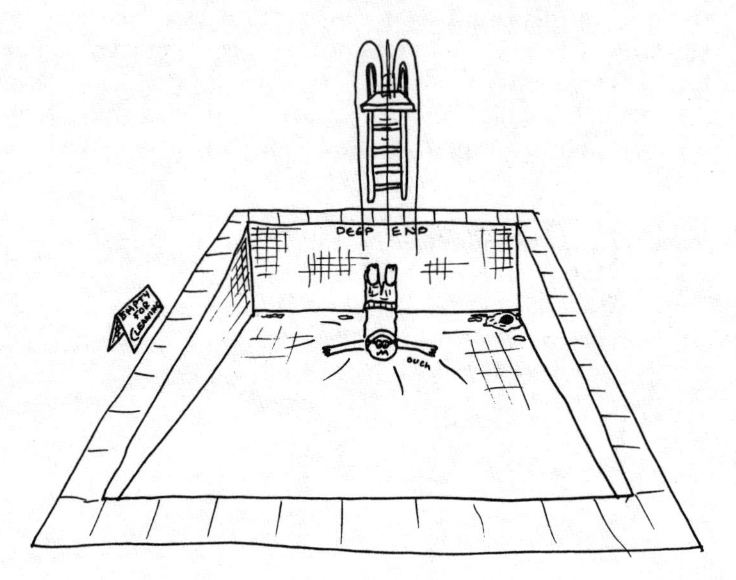

70. In at the Deep End

Bible reference: Romans 3:28

Teaching point: Doing Christian things does not make you a Christian—putting your faith in Jesus does

Equipment needed: A 'learn to swim' book from the local library; as much swimming equipment as you have, such as goggles, Bermuda shorts, flippers and a hat; a towel

Announce your intention to learn to swim. There is no time like the present! Put the equipment on over your clothes and show your book. Start to read it at a suitable place.

After a few leg and arm actions, make out that you are quite satisfied with your progress and think that you are now quite a good swimmer. It was easier than you thought it would be. Finish by saying how pleased you are that there was no need to go to the swimming pool as you are afraid of water. Take off your gear and roll it back into the towel. Look very pleased with yourself and ask the children if they are impressed.

Enter into a dialogue, asking what was wrong with your attempt to learn to swim. Is it possible to 'pretend' to be a Christian in the same way? In order to learn to swim you first have to get into the water. How do we start the Christian life? Perhaps some people try to do 'Christian strokes' like being good, going to church, saying their prayers and maybe even reading their Bibles. However, they have never given their lives to Jesus Christ. Is it possible to be afraid of trusting Jesus like people can be afraid of water? Just as doing swimming actions on dry land does not make you a swimmer, doing Christian things does not make you a Christian.

Songs: *I am a new creation* (SFK)
Hallelujah, my Father (SFK)
Happiness is to know the Saviour (JP)
We want to tell you of Jesus' love (SG)
Water of life (CP)

71. *'We Believe'*

Bible references: Hebrews 11:6; John 6:28–29

Teaching point: The most important thing God wants is faith in Jesus

Equipment needed: Overhead projector or blackboard

Ask the children to think about this question: 'What sort of person is God pleased with?'

Listen to their answers without making any comments. Then ask someone to look up and read John 6:28–29. Amazing! What God wants us to do is believe in the one he sent. Who was the one he sent? Of course, it was Jesus. If we believe in Jesus, we are doing exactly what God wants us to do.

Ask the children what they believe about Jesus, and write up their answers on the overhead projector. A few prompts may be needed to get a balanced set of statements. After they have finished, write at the top 'St Luke's Creed' (or whatever the name of your church, club or school is), and read your creed together. 'We believe . . . '

Songs: *We believe* (SFK)
Jesus Christ is alive today (JP)
There's no greater name than Jesus (SG)
The virgin Mary (CP)

72. *I Give Up*

Bible reference: Luke 19:1–10

Teaching point: Genuine repentance is an essential part of the Christian life

Equipment needed: An overhead projector or blackboard with a long sum written on it—eg, 491 + 437 − 283 × 7 + 16 = ?

Explain that there is some arithmetic you have to do before you are ready to start your talk. With a running commentary, start to do the sum, making several deliberate mistakes as you go along, and even guessing a few numbers. Insist it is not necessary to be exactly right all the way through, but give up when you are in a complete mess, with plenty of crossings-out and still no final total.

Admit defeat and ask some children to correct your mistakes and complete the sum. The others can check their answer.

Explain how everyone does lots of wrong things in their lives, sometimes accidentally, sometimes deliberately. Some people think that if they carry on and ignore these wrong things, everything will be all right in the end. Just as with the sum, this is not the case. Sins cannot be ignored—they have to be put right.

Tell or look up the story of Zacchaeus, noticing how he went back to where he had first gone wrong and made amends. Once he had done this, he was ready to live his life in the right way with Jesus as his Saviour. He had found salvation.

We too must put the past right by confessing our sins to God and saying sorry if we have hurt someone. We cannot just ignore our wrong-doings and hope that they will just get forgotten. That is not God's way.

Songs: *Nobody liked Zacchaeus* (SFK)
Let God speak (SFK)
Zacchaeus was a very little man (JP)
My Lord, my God, I know you see (SG)
Simple gifts (CP)

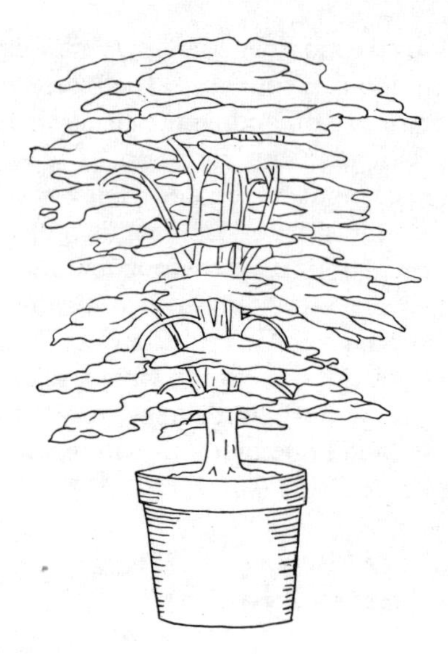

73. Bonsai

Bible references: Ephesians 3:17; Colossians 2:7; Psalm 1:3

Teaching point: The 'roots' of our lives need to be firmly embedded in Christ

Equipment needed: A bonsai (or a picture if a specimen is not available)

Start by asking, 'Did you know . . . ?' followed by this information: The largest living thing in the world is the giant redwood tree growing in the USA and Canada. It grows up to 112 metres in height—as tall as a thirty-storey building!

Show your bonsai, and see if anyone knows what it is called. Does anyone know why it is so small, even though it is fully grown?

Explain the principles of bonsai growing. The tree should be enormous, but because the roots are continually cut back, it grows in miniature.

The Bible says that those who believe in Jesus have, as it were, 'roots' which grow down into him. If our 'roots' are constantly clipped back, then we will not grow very much. Years may go by and we will still be at the beginning.

Ask for suggestions as to how to encourage our 'roots' to grow—such as: continuing to believe; putting our Christian lives into practice; praying; learning from the Bible; and having fellowship with other Christians. By doing these things, our 'roots' grow unseen. In time we will become like spiritual giant redwoods!

Songs: *I'm gonna say my prayers* (SFK)
If Jesus is de vine (SFK)
May the mind of Christ my Saviour (JP)
Walking with Jesus (SG)
Give us hope (CP)

74. *Ouch!*

Bible reference: 1 John 1:8–10

Teaching point: Continual confession of sins to God is essential for ongoing forgiveness and cleansing

Equipment needed: A local map; walking boots, one with a stone inside; a rucksack; a walking stick

As you gather your equipment together, talk about walking, pretending it is one of your favourite occupations. Give an imaginary outline of your intended expedition. Put on your boots and rucksack, say 'goodbye' and pretend to set off.

Before you get very far, the stone in your shoe should be very painful. Complain loudly and sit down. With exaggerated movements take off your shoe and tip out the stone.

Explain how the Christian life can be compared to a walk as

we follow Jesus each day. Sometimes we travel along quite happily, enjoying the presence and grace of God. From time to time, though, things crop up that make us aware of our sinful natures. This is like having a stone in our shoe. 'Stones' can be things like jealousy or selfishness. What other things can be like a stone? Just as it is impossible to continue walking with the stone, so in our Christian lives we need to stop and confess our sin to God. The Bible tells us that if we do this God forgives us immediately. Then we can walk on, full of his love and grace in our hearts.

(Not only do we receive his instant forgiveness, but God promises that he will secretly work in our hearts and change us for the better without us realising what is happening.)

Songs: *Change my heart, O God* (SFK)
I get so excited, Lord (SFK)
I want to walk with Jesus Christ (JP)(SFK)
Cleanse me (SG)
I've got peace like a river (CP)

75. *My Daddy*

Bible reference: Romans 8:15–16

Teaching point: Through Christ our relationship with God becomes so close that he is like our 'daddy'

Equipment needed: A list of the word 'Daddy' in as many different languages as possible. Here are some examples:

Vati – German
Tad – Welsh
Tata – Polish
Uba – Hausa (Nigerian language)
Abuna – Arabic
Baba – Turkish
Otosan – Japanese
Baa-baa – Cantonese

Papa	– French
Fa	– Danish
Pabbi	– Icelandic
Papas	– Greek
Appa	– Tamil (Indian language)
Pittha	– Nepali
Nana	– Telegu (Indian language)
Taata	– Runyankore (African language)
Bapaa	– Marathi (Indian language)

If any children present speak other languages, ask them to introduce themselves in their other language. Announce that you are going to learn lots of different languages! Display your word list.

Read down the list of words together, trying to pronounce them properly. Ask the younger ones if they can guess their meaning.

Look up Romans 8:15–16. The word 'Abba' is Aramaic for 'Daddy'. Jesus used this word when he talked to his heavenly Father. The Holy Spirit inside tells those who belong to Jesus that God is their 'daddy'.

Songs: *Father God, I wonder* (SFK)
Abba, Father (JP)(SFK)
Heavenly Father, may thy blessing (SG)(CP)

76. *My Big Brother*

Bible references: Matthew 12:46–50; Hebrews 2:11

Teaching point: Jesus' followers are his 'brothers'

Equipment needed: None

Ask if in the present company therc is a family with four members (if there are adults present, then ideally a mother and three sons). Invite them to come to the front. Alternatively, ask volunteers to play the parts of a small family. Select one of the family to play the part of Jesus and set him aside from the others.

Tell the family members to describe how they would feel now that one of them had become really famous like Jesus. Then ask for a volunteer to look up and read Matthew 12:46–50. Ask the family how they would feel if they had been rebuffed like that. Would they feel offended?

Why did Jesus respond in this way? What was in his mind?

Possibly he did not want to be interrupted while he was doing God's work. He used the opportunity to show how highly he regarded his followers and how important they were to him. They were just as important as his own family. Refer to Hebrews 2:11.

If we believe in Jesus, he thinks of us as his brothers and sisters!

Songs: *God is our Father* (SFK)
Brothers and sisters (JP)
Walking with Jesus (SG)
Jesus, good above all other (CP)

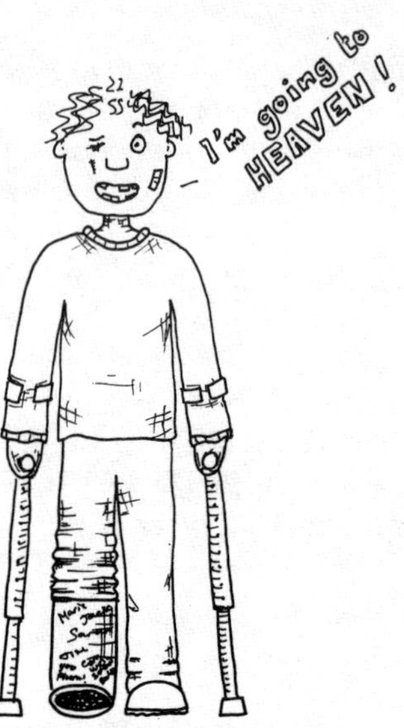

77. *Heaven, Here I Come!*

Bible references: Luke 10:20; 1 Peter 1:6

Teaching point: Present circumstances are as nothing compared to our eternal inheritance

Equipment needed: Five large cards with the following written on them:

1. Illness
2. Winning a large sum of money
3. Having your name written in heaven
4. Falling off your bike
5. Having your prayer answered

Ask if anyone can tell you what a 'multiple choice question' is. (It is when a person is asked to choose the correct answer from several given options.) Then present the following multiple choice question: 'What did Jesus and the apostle Peter tell us to rejoice and be glad about?'

Show your answer cards one by one, making no comment as you do so. Which is the correct answer? Come to a consensus as the choices are discussed.

The Bible references will confirm who was right. When the disciples were experiencing a thrilling time as they knew the power of God working through them, Jesus told them not to rejoice about this! Rather, they were to rejoice because their names were written in heaven. When things were going rather badly for the Christians Peter wrote to, he told them they should rejoice. They were not to rejoice about the problems, but to be glad because of the rich blessings which God had stored up for them in heaven.

So, whether things are good or bad, we rejoice! Good times may come and bad times may come, but we are on our way to heaven!

Songs: *O, heaven is in my heart* (SFK)
I will wave my hands (SFK)
I gotta home in gloryland (JP)
We are marching home (SG)
Rejoice in the Lord always (CP)

78. *None Are More Equal Than Others*

Bible reference:	Matthew 20:1–15
Teaching point:	The message of the parable of the workers in the vineyard—God is generous and treats us all alike
Equipment needed:	A tube of Smarties

Begin by asking the youngsters if they like to play 'Let's pretend'. What do they like to pretend to be? Talk about their favourite games for a while.

Do any of them ever pretend to be servants? Probably not! Announce that you are going to have a pretend game now and give out some jobs that some volunteers can pretend to do for you. Perhaps someone could pretend to clean your car. Someone else could pretend to cook your dinner. Others could make your bed, tidy your bookshelves, iron your clothes or whatever. Come prepared with a list relevant to your situation. Finally, ask the rest to pretend to hang up your coat. Then call a halt to the proceedings, and announce that it is time for the payments to be made for the work done. Everybody receives one Smartie.

Talk about what has taken place and ask whether the children think it is fair that everybody received the same.

Recap or tell the parable of the workers in the vineyard, in Matthew 20:1–15. We receive God's goodness because he is generous, not because we earned it.

Songs: *We will praise* (SFK)
O Lord, you're great (SFK)
You can't stop the rain (JP)(SG)(CP)

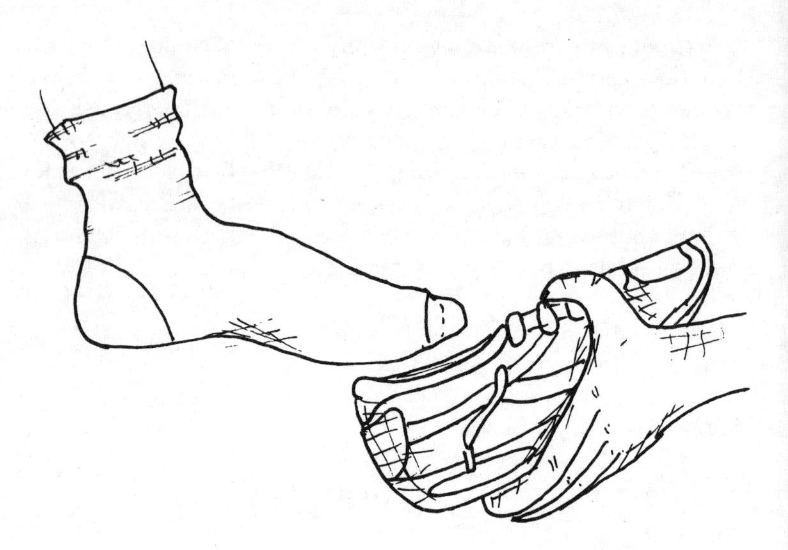

79. *All Indians and No Chiefs*

Bible references: Luke 22:24–27; John 13:1–17

Teaching point: The truth that each Christian is to be a humble servant of others

Equipment needed: None

Call up all the children present and divide them into two equal groups: older and younger.

Ask the younger group to take off their shoes, put one in one corner of the room, the other in another corner, then return to their seats. Ask the older ones to collect one pair each, then fit them back on the right person.

Once the exercise is completed, ask the children if they know what one of the tasks was that only the lowest servant would do in the time of Jesus. The answer is: washing other people's feet. This was always done by servants. Why did Jesus wash his disciples' feet just before his death?

Jesus wants us to have servant hearts and do servant tasks for one another.

Songs: *From heav'n you came* (SFK)
A new commandment (SFK)
Make me a channel of your peace (SFK)(JP)(CP)
Like Jesus (SG)

80. *A Little Is a Lot*

Bible references: Luke 21:1–4; 6:38

Teaching point: God wants us to be generous givers

Equipment needed: Four pieces of cardboard cut out in the shape of a purse, with either £1, 50p, £40 or 2p written on them; 10p, 2p, £1 and two 1p coins; an offering basket or bag

Ask for four volunteers to face the front. Give each one a cardboard purse, making sure everyone can see how much they have in their purses by the amount shown on the front. Give them 10p, 2p, £1 and two times 1p respectively, then ask them to show these amounts before putting them into an offering basket or bag which will be passed in front of them.

Once this has happened, ask the others to work out which one of these volunteers gave the most. The answer, of course, is the one who gave the biggest proportion and not who gave the largest amount.

Read or tell the story in Luke 21:1–4. Which of your four volunteers is like the widow? Who did Jesus say gave the most?

Finish by looking at Luke 6:38. We can afford to be generous, because God is so generous to us. What an amazing promise to those who give!

Songs: *Jesus, you gave everything* (SFK)
Change my heart (SFK)
I have decided to follow Jesus (JP)(SFK)
All that I have (SG)
Heavenly Father, may thy blessing (CP)(SG)

81. More Than Feelings

Bible references: James 2:14–17; 2 Corinthians 1:3–4

Teaching point: To encourage compassionate action

Equipment needed: Ten cards, each with one of the letters of the word 'compassion' on them

Give the cards at random to ten volunteers, asking them to make a single word out of the letters and then stand themselves in a straight line so that everyone else can see it. (With a small group, give the whole group the letters to sort out.)

Once assembled, ask what the word 'compassion' means. Examine the emotions that accompany a feeling of compassion. Ask the youngsters to describe some situations where a person may feel compassion. However, feeling sorry is not enough. Read the Bible passage.

Use one of the situations mentioned by the youngsters, or a local circumstance known to everyone, and ask for suggested actions that can be taken—things like: pray; give money; give help; and write letters. True compassion always leads to action.

Songs: *I will speak out* (SFK)
Soften my heart (SFK)
Kum ba yah (SG)(JP)(CP)
Make me a channel of your peace (SFK)(JP)(CP)

82. *Anything You Ask*

Bible references: John 14:13–14; 15:16

Teaching point: God has promised to answer prayers prayed in Jesus' name

Equipment needed: Overhead projector or blackboard on which is drawn an empty music stave—five lines with the treble clef at the beginning; a descant recorder

Make conversation about great composers of music. Then ask if there is anyone present who could compose a simple tune. Ask the volunteer to have a go using your music stave.

As this is happening, explain that you need to know a bit about music before you can write a tune. It is no good just writing a jumble of notes hoping they might sound all right. When the tune is ready, ask for another volunteer to try to play it on the recorder.

Refer to John 14:13–14 and John 15:16. These verses tell us that we will receive whatever we ask for in Jesus' name. Just as the music was written by one person and played by another, so we write the music (by asking God for things in the name of Jesus) and God plays our tune (by answering us and giving us those things). The more we learn about music, the more we can compose. The more we grow as Christians, the more we have faith to ask.

Songs: *Prayer is like a telephone* (SFK)
My God is so big (JP)(SFK)
Ask, ask, ask (SG)
Come and praise the Lord our King (CP)

83. *Wonderful Washing Up!*

Bible references: 1 Corinthians 10:31; Matthew 25:40; Colossians 3:17

Teaching point: Everything we do should be done for the glory of God

Equipment needed: A bowl of washing-up water; cups; rubber gloves; an apron; a tea-towel; protective covering for table if necessary

Carry the bowl into position, put on the rubber gloves and apron, sigh deeply, put the cups in the bowl and begin to wash them in turn.

Moan loudly about how boring life is. Pretend to feel very sorry for yourself. Your monologue could go something like this: 'Here I am washing up the church cups yet again. I have been washing up cups at the rate of about ten a day for at least ten years. That equals 365, times 10, times 10. I have washed up 36,500 cups in my life! This is such depressing news.'

Arrange beforehand for the relevant parts of the above Bible verses to be read out as you begin to dry the cups.

Look up and listen carefully. Say that perhaps there is a different way of thinking about washing up cups that you have not thought of before. You have washed up 36,500 cups as if you were doing it for Jesus!

Resume the task with much more enthusiasm and energy. It is a very important and significant job after all.

With a big smile on your face, rehearse a list of other similar jobs as you carry out the cups and bowl of water.

Songs: *Lord, help me to joyfully praise* (SFK)
The greatest thing in all my life (JP)
Heavenly Father may thy blessing (SG)(CP)
One more step (CP)

84. *Interest Rates Up*

Bible reference: Matthew 6:19–21

Teaching point: We should store up treasures in heaven, not on earth

Equipment needed: Large sheets of paper with 'Royal Bank of Heaven—Deposit' written on them; rubber stamp (optional); Bible references on postcards

See if the children can name some high street banks. What is a bank account? Explain how money is deposited into and drawn from an account.

Refer to the Bible reference in Matthew 6:19–21. How do we store up 'treasures on earth'? By putting more and more money in our bank accounts, or buying more and more things. We need to use our money with faith, not to pamper ourselves.

How do we store up 'treasures in heaven'? What does this mean? What do we have to do? Give out the Bible references:

John 3:16	(believe)
Matthew 19:29	(make sacrifices)
James 1:12	(don't give up)
Matthew 5:11–12	(be insulted)
Matthew 10:32	(speak openly about Jesus)
Matthew 6:6	(pray when you are alone)
Hebrews 6:10; Matthew 25:34–36	(show love for others in practical ways)

After each one is read out, ask: 'What is the treasure that can be deposited in heaven?' Choose a volunteer to come and fill in a Royal Bank of Heaven deposit slip. Pretend to be the cashier and stamp or sign it as it is paid in.

Jesus tells us there is a terrific rate of interest on our heavenly deposits and they never grow old or lose their value!

Songs: *O, heaven is in my heart* (SFK)
Lord, you are more precious (SFK)
Jesus, how lovely you are (JP)(SFK)
Here we come with gladness (SG)
At the name of Jesus (CP)(JP)

85. *Seventy Times Seven*

Bible reference: Matthew 18:21–22

Teaching point: Forgiving others is extremely important

Equipment needed: A pile of blank acetates and non-permanent marker pens

Put a blank acetate on the overhead projector and begin to write out the song which you have chosen to be sung afterwards, pretending that you have not had enough time to prepare properly for the talk. Make immediate blots or mistakes and start again with clean acetates. Do this quite quickly so that you discard five acetates in no time at all.

Make exasperated noises and comments as you go along. Continue the exercise just long enough for your audience to begin to get impatient with you. Ask someone to look up Matthew 18:21–22 while you have yet another try. Keep going while these verses are read, finally giving up as the reading finishes.

Is anyone getting impatient with you? You still have not finished. How many times did Jesus say we were to forgive one another?

We all get annoyed with each other at times, but as God is very forgiving towards us it is only right that we keep on forgiving others, whether they have sinned against us in big ways or small.

Using a pre-prepared acetate, sing the song you were attempting to write out earlier.

Songs: *God forgave my sin* (SFK)(JP)
Love, love your enemies (SFK)
Like Jesus (SG)
Make me a channel of your peace (CP)

86. Be Generous

Bible references: Luke 8:1–3; Matthew 25:40; Acts 4:32

Teaching point: God wants us to be generous with our possessions

Equipment needed: A list of everyday small items which the children are likely to have with them—eg, 10p piece, handkerchief, belt; Smarties or similar sweets as prizes (optional)

Begin by playing a game with your list of objects, asking for the first person to come forward with each item that you call out. If desired, reward each winner.

Move on to larger objects which the children might have at home, this time asking for hands to be raised in response, such as a large garden, certain toys or a computer.

Then look up Luke 8:1–3 and briefly explain the passage. We

are not told in what way these ladies helped Jesus. Do the children have any ideas? (Maybe providing bed and breakfast, or washing clothes, or preparing food for journeys.) Some of them must have been quite well off.

Is it possible to give our resources to Jesus today, now he has returned to heaven? We can do this by sharing them with or giving them away to others. When we do this, it is as though we are giving them to Jesus himself.

Songs: *Here I am, Lord* (SFK)
Father, we adore you (SFK)
Jesus, I will come with you (JP)
Who can? (SG)
Let the world rejoice together (CP)

87. *Who Comes First?*

Bible reference: James 2:1–9

Teaching point: We must not consider some people more important than others

Equipment needed: A letter inside a sealed, expensive looking envelope, and one inside a small manila envelope; a mirror and comb in your pocket

Begin your talk by taking the letters out of your pocket, pretending that you have not had time to open them. One looks terribly exciting so you are sure no one will mind if you open it now.

Read the first letter and pretend to be amazed. It is an invitation from the mayor to attend a civic reception. He is giving a free lunch to thank all those in the town who have given valuable service. How exciting! You have never been honoured in such a way before. Take the mirror out of your pocket and look at yourself in it. Take out the comb and comb your hair with a self-important look.

Continue by idly opening the second letter and look rather annoyed as you read its contents. Explain that a previous neighbour, whom you haven't seen for years and never really got on with, is getting married, and you are invited to the wedding. There is to be a simple civil ceremony followed by a cup of tea. You have been invited to say a prayer of blessing. Complain that it will take over an hour to drive there, you will have to buy a wedding present and there will be no one there whom you know. Look at the date with horror. It is exactly the same time as the mayor's reception.

Ask the children which one you should go to and why. Which one would they go to and why? Which one do they think Jesus would go to and why?

Songs: *Jesus, you gave everything* (SFK)
I will love you, Lord (SFK)
Make me a servant (JP)
The Bible tells of God's great plan (SG)
Make me a channel of your peace (CP)

88. *We're in the Lord's Army*

Bible references: Ephesians 6:11–18; Revelation 19:11–16

Teaching point: Christians are part of a spiritual army fighting against evil

Equipment needed: Cardboard or paper cut-outs of soldiers with the words 'unbelief', 'lies', 'despair', 'violence' and 'wickedness' written on them

If speaking to a church, ask any soldiers, ex-soldiers, cadets, Territorial Army members or would-be soldiers in the congregation to come out and do some 'square-bashing'. (You're at an advantage if you have members of Boys' or Girls' Brigades!) Alternatively, ask for a few volunteers and march them around the room yourself.

Did the children know that as Christians we are 'conscripted' into the spiritual army of Jesus? Jesus and his army are engaged in a battle. Give the cardboard cut-outs to your recruits and describe these enemies of Christ.

What possible weapons can we use to defeat enemies such as these? What do we use to overcome unbelief or despair? Evil is to be overcome with spiritual weapons.

Look at the Bible passage in Ephesians and link in with the cardboard cut-outs. End on a note of triumph. Jesus promises that we will be the conquerors, not the conquered. There is no need to fear with Christ as our commander.

Songs: *So we're marching along* (SFK)
Not by might (SFK)
I can run through a troop (JP)
We are marching home to heaven (SG)
In the bustle of the city (CP)

89. *Keep Going!*

Bible references: Matthew 25:1–13; Galatians 6:9

Teaching point: Perseverance and patience are essential

Equipment needed: A clockwork toy

Wind up the toy and set it in motion so that everyone can see it. When it winds down, pick it up, wind it up and repeat the process. Comment on how fascinating these toys can be. Talk about them having one big problem, but give no hint as to what that problem might be.

Sigh, and say that Christians can have a similar problem.

Jesus told a parable about this problem. Tell the story of the ten girls at the wedding found in Matthew 25:1–13. Five of the girls ran out of steam!

Our human nature likes everything to be 'instant' and 'straight away', and we do not like having to be patient! The clockwork toy only keeps going for such a short time. The girls who ran out of oil missed the bridegroom. Those who were prepared for a long wait got their reward!

Songs: *Don't be lazy* (SFK)
So I've made up my mind (SFK)
I have decided to follow Jesus (JP)
We are marching home to heaven (SG)
Jesus, good above all other (CP)

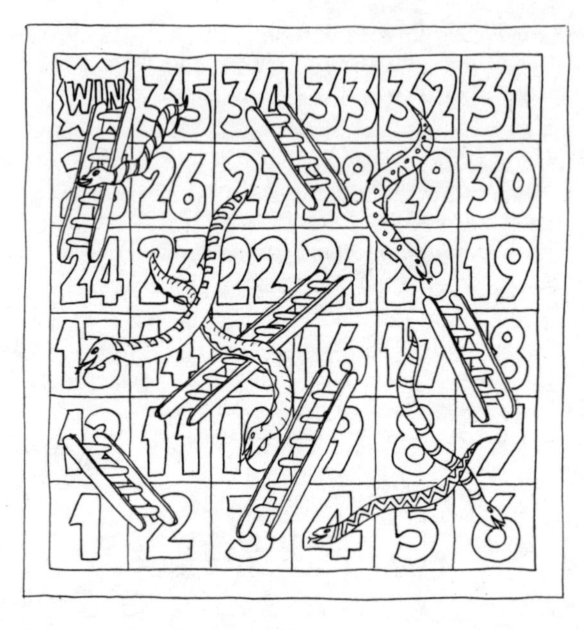

90. *Snakes and Ladders*

Bible references: Matthew 24:13; Acts 14:22

Teaching point: Perseverance is essential in the face of difficulties

Equipment needed: The game of snakes and ladders drawn onto an overhead projector slide or blackboard (or a board for a small group—a board with 100 squares will take longer); for the dice: six small cards numbered one to six inside a bag; one can be drawn out and immediately replaced; two bags will facilitate play if numbers are large; two different shapes to mark the progress of the two teams

Divide everyone into two teams for a game of snakes and ladders.

Explain how the 'dice' will work. Choose two volunteers to move the markers on the board, and another volunteer to take the 'dice bag' between the two teams, then begin.

The game should be fairly quick moving if the numbers are selected in quick rotation. At fairly regular intervals, especially when one team goes down a snake, say something like: 'Why don't we give up?' or 'Shall we stop there?' Hopefully, your audience will reply in the negative!

When one team has won the game, explain how life can seem like a game of snakes and ladders, with many ups and downs. When things go wrong the disappointment can be very painful. It hurts slipping down a snake. However, the important thing is not to give up. In snakes and ladders when we slip down a snake we keep going and eventually we pass the place where we went down. We may go down the same snake twice, but sooner or later we will pass it. Similarly, when disappointments and failures come our way in real life, as they surely will, we must not give up.

Jesus never promised that life would be easy, but he promised that everyone who finishes gets a wonderful reward in heaven!

Songs: *We're stepping out in power* (SFK)
Big man (SFK)(JP)
I want to walk with Jesus Christ (JP)(SFK)
Follow, follow, I would follow Jesus (SG)
I am planting my feet (CP)

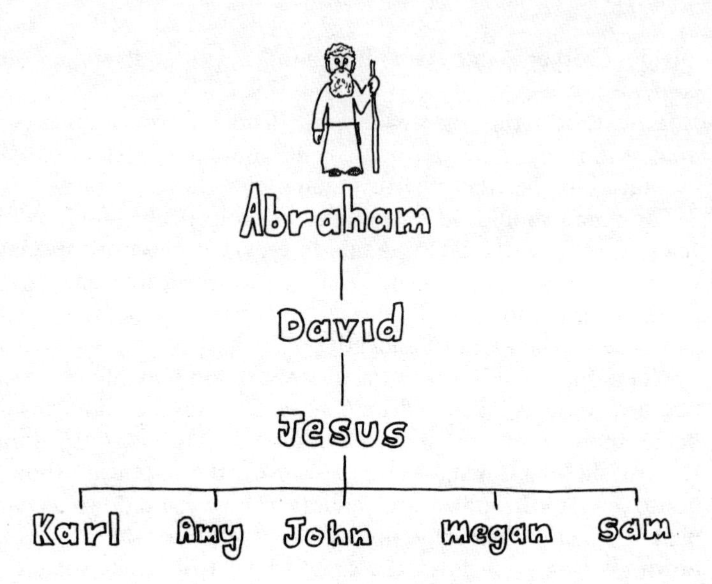

91. *The Biggest Grandad of Them All*

Bible references: Genesis 13:16; Romans 4:16; Galatians 3:7

Teaching point: Through faith in Christ we are descendants of Abraham

Equipment needed: An overhead projector or blackboard

Begin by explaining that 4,000 years ago God chose a man called Abraham and told him that he would be the father of many descendants. Read Genesis 13:16.

Ask the children what a family tree is. Ask for one or two to name their fathers and grandfathers and draw a quick example on the overhead projector or blackboard.

Do the children know who is in Abraham's family tree? Draw up the family tree illustrated, or have it prepared already using the names of some of the people present.

Everyone who has faith in Jesus is a descendant of Abraham! Refer to Galatians 3:7. We are related to him in Christ.

Songs: *Father Abraham had many sons* (SFK)
God is working his purpose out (JP)
I am so glad (SG)
God has promised (CP)

92. *All Change!*

Bible references: 1 Corinthians 15:51–52; 1 Thessalonians 4:15–17; John 11:25; 5:28

Teaching point: When Jesus comes again, all believers who are now dead will rise to life, and we who are alive will be given new bodies

Equipment needed: Large cardboard cut-out butterfly wings, painted or decorated simply for you to wear—staple or tape cardboard straps on the inside to hold wings in place on your wrists and arms; a leafy branch of a plant or bush

Wear green or brown, and when you are ready to begin your talk pull on a green or brown woolly hat if you have one. The aim is to look like a caterpillar! Make sure the wings are to hand but out of sight.

Pretend to chew the leaves and talk about what an ugly fat caterpillar you are. It is hard to believe, but one day soon you will turn into a beautiful creature.

How could it be possible for a caterpillar to change into a butterfly as the two are not in the least bit alike? What are some of the differences between a caterpillar and a butterfly?

During your monologue, talk about how Christians can be compared to caterpillars. The Bible says they will be transformed in 'the twinkling of an eye' and will suddenly find themselves with different bodies. Maybe we will even be able to fly, as we will go up into the air to meet Jesus! It sounds impossible. But is it any more impossible for a caterpillar to change into a butterfly?

Finally, tell everyone to close their eyes. If you have a trumpet player available, he or she could play a fanfare. While this is happening, slip on your wings and hold out your arms horizontally, your back turned to the audience so that the wings can be clearly seen. It has happened. The caterpillar has changed into a butterfly!

It will happen. We will all be changed!

Songs: *What a wonderful Saviour is Jesus* (SFK)(JP)(SG)
When the trumpet of the Lord (JP)
When he comes (SG)

SECTION EIGHT

Special Occasions

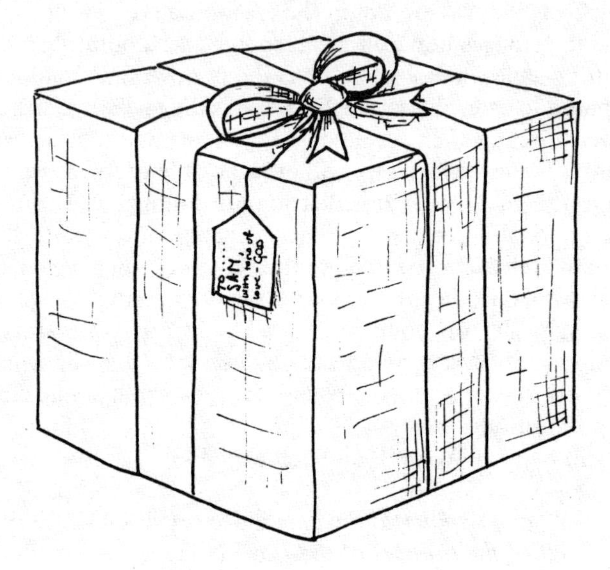

93. *Just What I Needed (Christmas)*

Bible reference: Matthew 1:21,23

Teaching point: Jesus was given by God as the perfect gift for mankind

Equipment needed: A Christmas box or parcel with a gift tag inscribed 'to . . . ' (insert your own name) and 'From God'; inside the box put a large piece of paper with the name 'Jesus' written on it

Begin your talk by asking who is looking forward to Christmas, and what presents are expected or have been received. Talk about your own presents in a disappointed way. Complain about your bathroom being full of unwanted soaps and your bedroom full of unwanted socks. Presents can look exciting but can be disappointing when you actually open them.

Arrange beforehand for someone to pass you your prepared present. Read out the label and notice that it says 'From God'. If anyone should give you something you really want, it should be God as he knows you inside out. This present should be something extra special. Build up a sense of anticipation as you open it.

Look inside the box, put your hand in and bring out the piece of paper. Read out the word 'Jesus' slowly and deliberately. Look absolutely thrilled and say something like: 'Jesus, just for me!'

Explain that many people don't think that Jesus is very exciting, but he is the best possible gift anyone could ever receive. There are two reasons for this:

First, what does Matthew 1:21 say about Jesus?—'He will save his people from their sins.' More than anything else you need someone to save you from your sins. Secondly, what does Matthew 1:23 say about Jesus?—'He shall be called Emmanuel, which means, God with us.' More than anything else, you need God to be with you all the time. Jesus is perfect for each one of us. Our two greatest needs are met by him: to be forgiven by God, and to be with him for ever.

Songs: *The sky is filled* (SFK)
Calypso carol (JP)(SG)

94. *Here He Comes! (Palm Sunday)*

Bible reference: Matthew 21:1–11

Teaching point: To convey some of the excitement of Palm Sunday

Equipment needed: Some coconut shells, or plastic beakers, to sound like a donkey's hooves; wooden rulers to strike the back of a chair; paper for rustling noises; 'auto-cue' cards (see below); a microphone to highlight the hoof sounds (optional)

Begin by telling the Palm Sunday story in as exciting way as possible, commenting on how noisy the occasion must have been. Ask the children to point out some of the different noises that were heard as Jesus rode into Jerusalem.

Suggest that together you should make an 'audio presentation', recreating the sounds that would have been made on the first Palm Sunday.

Give one volunteer the coconut shells for the 'clip-clop' of the donkey. Another one or two hit the back of a chair with wooden rulers to make the sound of branches being torn from the trees. Other volunteers can flap sheets of paper to sound like branches waving. Everyone can shuffle their feet to sound like a crowd approaching when this auto-cue is chosen. Ask the rest to shout 'Hosanna to the Son of David', 'Blessed is he who comes in the name of the Lord' and 'Hosanna in the highest', according to the auto-cue chosen. Finally, choose someone to call out 'Who is this?' In reply, everyone is to shout 'This is Jesus, the prophet from Nazareth in Galilee.'

Once all the parts have been given out the leader will need to conduct the presentation by pointing to the different volunteers in turn, starting with the clip-clop. Use the auto-cues to bring in the shouts at various intervals.

To bring things to a conclusion, an appropriate Palm Sunday song can be sung, such as 'Hosanna'.

Songs: *Hosanna* (SFK)
Children of Jerusalem (JP)
What do I see? (SG)
Trotting, trotting (CP)

95. The Price of a Slave (Good Friday)

Bible references: Exodus 21:32; Matthew 26:14–16

Teaching point: Jesus was betrayed for thirty pieces of silver, which was the price of a slave

Equipment needed: Some items of varying value—eg, a painting, some jewellery, a popular children's toy

Ask the children to put a price on each of your articles. Come to a consensus about how much each one is worth.

Ask a young man to come forward. Explain the principle of slavery. How much would a young man like this be worth as a slave? Think together about how much it would cost to feed him and how much work he would do. Refer to Exodus 21:32. The verse explains that a slave was sold for thirty pieces of silver. This was equivalent to about one month's wages.

Someone very famous was sold for that amount. Who was it?

The answer of course is Jesus (see Matthew 26:14–16). How could the Son of God be sold for the price of a slave? Jesus took the very lowest place in society when he gave up his life.

Songs: *From heav'n you came* (SFK)
What a wonderful Saviour (JP)(SFK)
It is a thing most wonderful (SG)
Jesus in the garden (CP)

96. He Is Risen Indeed (Easter Sunday)

Bible references: Luke 24; John 20

Teaching point: Jesus physically rose from the dead

Equipment needed: Two large signs, one reading 'possible' and the other 'impossible'

Your plan is to ask a number of questions to which the answer will be either 'impossible' or 'possible'. Show the two cards and get two volunteers to come and hold up whichever one the audience calls out. Be prepared with your list of questions. Here are some examples:

Can a fish live out of water?
Can a person get younger instead of older?

Can a person make a million pounds starting from just one pound?

Can a person turn his or her head 360 degrees?

You might like to look in the *Guiness Book of Records* for some unlikely stories which are actually true.

Your final question will be: Can a dead person live again?

God did the impossible by raising his Son Jesus from the dead.

Ask those who believe this to raise their hands.

Lead the congregation in a shout: 'Christ is risen! Hallelujah!'

Songs: *Led like a lamb* (SFK)
He is Lord (JP)(SFK)
Low in the grave he lay (SG)(JP)
All in an Easter garden (CP)

97. *What Superb Timing! (Harvest Thanksgiving)*

Bible references: Psalm 104; Genesis 1:12; 8:22

Teaching point: God created the plant kingdom with fantastic precision and skill

Equipment needed: An apple; a clock; a large card with the word 'photoperiodism' on it

Pick up an apple and ask if anyone has an apple tree in his or her garden. Ask if anyone knows when it blossoms.

It is crucial for the tree to blossom in spring so that there are insects to pollinate it and so that the fruit can grow during the warm summer months. How do trees know that spring has arrived? They never make a mistake. God has put a clock inside each one! Not the type of clock we usually think of—something more like a microscopic computer program.

Amazingly, the tree is sensitive to the hours of daylight. It counts the hours of daylight to the accuracy of a few minutes! When the daytime reaches exactly the right length, tiny genes signal to the tree to start producing its flowers. This ability in plants to respond to daylight hours has a long name. Hold up the word and see if anyone can read it. Practise saying it together for fun.

What would happen without photoperiodism? There would be no harvest! Read Genesis 8:22. God decided upon the seasons and he made sure the plants obeyed his rules! He put his clock inside them! What chaos there would be if seasons got out of control. Without spring-time there would be no harvest.

Songs: *He made the earth* (SFK)
Think of a world without (JP)(CP)
We plough the fields (SG)

98. *Baby-talk (Christening or Dedication)*

Bible reference: Psalm 8:2

Teaching point: A new-born baby shows the greatness of God

Equipment needed: None

New-born babies speak a message! How can that be when they do not know how to talk? What noise do new-born babies make? They cry! What are they telling us when they cry?—'I want Mummy,' or 'I want food.'

The Bible tells us that their crying contains another message; quite a different one. Look at Psalm 8:2. The noise they make is praise to God! How funny! How can this make sense? The very fact that they can cry means that they are alive. Every new life is a miracle of God's handiwork and creation. So the cry of every new-born baby is a declaration of the greatness of God!

Songs: *He made the earth* (SFK)
All around me, Lord (JP)
All things bright and beautiful (SG)(JP)(CP)
When God made the garden of creation (CP)

99. *Can God Forget Us? (Mother's Day)*

Bible reference: Isaiah 49:14–16

Teaching point: God loves his people more than mothers love their children

Equipment needed: None

If speaking in a church, choose some mothers in the congregation, or ask for some volunteers. Interview them one by one, asking them questions like these:

How many children do you have?
Are your children on your mind all the time?
Could you imagine ever forgetting your children?
Do you have a favourite memory?

Do you love your grandchildren as though they were your own children?

How has becoming a mother changed your life?

How do you feel if your child misbehaves?

Read out the Bible reference and compare God's love with the love of these mothers.

Songs: *I'm special* (SFK)(JP)
You can't stop the rain (SG)(CP)(JP)

100. Our Father (Father's Day)

Bible reference: Romans 8:15–16

Teaching point: God becomes our Father when we put our faith in Jesus, his Son; we know this by the indwelling presence of the Holy Spirit

Equipment needed: None

If speaking in a church, ask those fathers whose children are present to come forward and be your visual aid. Stand them in a line facing the congregation.

Then ask the children whose fathers have come forward to get ready. Organise the children into a line to file past these fathers, stopping when they reach their own.

Fathers usually stretch out their arms, or give an affectionate welcome when their child approaches. Make comments on the love that is shown.

With everyone still in position, use the Bible reference to explain how God becomes our heavenly Father when we believe in Jesus, and that 'Abba' is a very affectionate word for him, rather like 'Daddy'. Some people do not have a father. However, everyone can have the best daddy of all.

Songs: *Father* (SFK)
Father God, I wonder (SFK)
Heavenly Father, may thy blessing (JP)(SG)
You can't stop the rain (CP)(JP)(SG)

Scripture Index